For the first tim
the title of a book is selected through
online public voting

Dr APJ Abdul Kalam, one of the most remarkable leaders of contemporary India, is an extremely popular public figure. He has 1.8 million people following him on Facebook and receives about 300 emails everyday. His active and visible presence on the social media provided a unique opportunity to engage with his readers in a way that has never been done before. Dr Kalam shortlisted 5 titles for this book which were put online for twelve days and people were asked to vote for the title they liked the most. A staggering 41,675 people sent in their votes and the title, **Forge Your Future**, got the maximum number of votes. And that is how this book got its title!

Forge Your Future provides an insight into the issues which concern and engage the minds of young Indians. As Dr Kalam writes in the Introduction to this book, "The wide spectrum of issues reflected in the book are like the colours of the rainbow, each one different from the other, but all emanating from one light. And that one light is the illumination of the soul, the honesty, the hope and the curiosity radiating through the minds of our young people. Through this book I want to keep alive and shining bright, the light in the minds and souls of our youth, and inspire them to reach great heights of achievement."

Avul Pakir Jainulabdeen Abdul Kalam is a simple, down-to-earth man who believes in marrying the goodness of the human spirit with the power of technology for maximizing good for the human race. **Indomitable Spirit, Ignited Minds, Wings of Fire, Turning Points, Spirit of India** and **Inspiring Thoughts** are some of his bestselling books which have captivated the hearts of millions of his readers.

FORGE
YOUR FUTURE

APJ Abdul Kalam

rajpal

1912-2012
100 Years of
Excellence in Publishing

rajpal

₹ **250**

ISBN : 978-93-5064-279-5

Revised Edition : 2014, Ist Reprint : 2014

© APJ Abdul Kalam

FORGE YOUR FUTURE (Inspiration & Personal Growth)

by APJ Abdul Kalam

Cover picture courtesy : Samar Mondol, Rashtrapati Bhawan

Printed at G.H. Prints, Delhi

RAJPAL & SONS

1590, Madarsa Road, Kashmere Gate, Delhi-110006

Phone : 011-23869812, 23865483, Fax : 011-23867791

website : www.rajpalpublishing.com

e-mail : sales@rajpalpublishing.com

To all my
young friends
who find the time to
write to me

Contents

Thanksgiving

For several years now, a team of dedicated persons is working with me, tirelessly and selflessly. They assist me in preparing my lectures and travel with me, wherever I go. Their meticulous recordings and notings of the responses and feelings of the hundreds and thousands of people with whom I interact, provides an invaluable base for me to later reflect upon, and articulate my learnings. I often wonder, what motivates them! I have yet to find a definitive answer and so I guess it is their loving kindness which resonates with me.

I thank each one of them - Sheridon, Prasad, Dhan Shyam, Ponraj and General Swaminathan. Unfortunately, General Swaminathan passed away before this book could be published.

My friend Prof Arun Tiwari, along with Dhan Shyam Sharma, made specific contributions to this book. Dhan Shyam Sharma read through thousands of mails and organised them into neat thought-domains. Arun diligently merged many mails for better comprehension and helped shape my thoughts into sentences.

I am happy to work with Rajpal & Sons, particularly Meera Johri, on this book.

I learnt from my parents that the very quality of our life, whether we love it or hate it, is based upon how thankful we are towards God. I thank all the millions of my young friends who find the time to write to me and post their questions.

The true measure of our thanksgiving is not what we say about our blessings, but how we use them. So, I thank you, my reader, for picking up this book amidst the thousands of distractions floating around in the physical and cyber space.

I pray for each one of you, that may all your misgivings be transformed into thanksgivings.

–APJ Abdul Kalam

New Delhi
August 2014

Introduction

In the last fifteen years I have interacted with 16 million youth, in face-to-face meetings, through email and over Facebook. Wherever I go I am asked questions. There are 1.8 million people following me on Facebook and on an average I receive 300 emails a day and spend about two hours daily reading and answering them.

This book is based on the questions that I have been asked over the years. From the hundreds of thousands of mails in my inbox it was very difficult to decide which should be included in this book and which should be left out. The mails you find here provide a unique insight into the issues which concern and engage the minds of young Indians. The wide spectrum of issues reflected in these are like the colours of the rainbow, each one different from the other, but all emanating from one light. And that one light is the illumination of the soul, the honesty, hope and curiosity radiating through the minds of our young people. Through this book I want to keep alive and shining bright, the light in the minds and souls of our youth, and inspire them to reach great heights of achievement.

Through their mails, the youth are seeking solutions to problems that they are facing in their lives. Answering these questions led to the realisation that what we call problems are probably a result of the way we 'process' our lives and all that which happens in our world. 'Process' means the way we perceive and think about the events in our life. If we could change the way we 'process' the situations and events, we could possibly change the way we think about our problems and hence also their solutions. Is it possible to learn to process in a different way? I strongly believe it is possible and that is what I have attempted in my answers to the questions.

My replies to the questions are based on my personal life-experiences and all that I have learnt from reading books and my interactions with political and spiritual leaders. The replies are presented in a way that they become generic messages for all those readers who may be facing similar problems or situations in their lives.

As you read, you will realise that most of my replies call for focusing attention on what we intend to manifest at this moment in our life. When we do that, when we put our full attention and concentration on that and act upon it, we attract more of *what we want*, rather than attracting more of *what we do not want*. One of the reasons most people are not good at solving problems is because their thoughts are always on the problem instead of being on the solution.

Despite the fact that I spent my childhood in Rameswaram, an isolated island in the south of India, I could get educated, find a job and overcome many obstacles to become the President of my country. If I could overcome the hardships and achieve what I have, so can you or anyone else. Today I spend much of my time communicating with the youth of our country, through my speeches, books and travels across the nation and abroad, talking to them, motivating them to do the same. I always tell them to focus on the solution and not the problem, because you need to focus all your energy on where you want to be and not where you currently are.

Your life should be a manifestation of your dreams. That is why I always call upon the youth to dream lofty dreams and invoke in them a vision of their future. And in achieving your dreams, you are bound to face difficulties and obstacles, but with determination and discipline you can always overcome them, just as I have been able to do.

There is a hymn in the *Brihadaranyaka Upanishad*:

असतो मा सद्गमय;
तमसो मा ज्योतिर्गमय;
मृत्योर्मा अमृतं गमय।

From ignorance, lead me to truth
From darkness, lead me to light
From death, lead me to immortality

These lines convey that falsehood and darkness lead to low energy levels, but when you bring the higher energies of truth, light and spiritual immortality into the presence of lower energy levels, the latter simply cannot survive. Just as truth eliminates falsehood, light dissolves darkness, and after death the soul becomes immortal, in the same way, love dissolves hate, joy dissolves sadness and faith dissolves doubt. And once we begin to put our problems into that context, we can bring to bear the higher energies of love, kindness and forgiveness to our problems and dissolve them. As I said, it is a matter of changing our mind about how we are going to process the information and events in our lives.

As a student, I was very fortunate to have been taught by caring and inspiring teachers such as Muthu Iyer, Siva Subramania Iyer, Iyadurai Solomon and Thothatri Iyengar and later in my professional life I had the opportunity work with great people like Vikram Sarabhai, Satish Dhawan and three Prime Ministers. When you walk into the presence of people who operate at the highest energy levels, by just being in their energy field, everything that is diseased or in disharmony, is healed. When you bring a higher and a more loving energy into the presence of disorder, disharmony or disease, you are really bringing a healing energy.

Everyone and everything in this world is connected, and those who live at very high and fast energy levels are able to compensate for people who live at very low and slow energies. There is a wonderful book about this called, *Power vs. Force,* by David Hawkins, a medical doctor, which explains the counter-balancing effect of people with higher energies on people who operate at very low energies. It says that on a scale of one to 1,000, with 1,000 representing divine unity consciousnesses and a one representing the lowest energy, that one person at 1,000, let's say someone like Mahatma Gandhi or Nelson Mandela, would counter-balance the negativity of everybody else on the planet.

It is not that people such as Mahatma Gandhi or Nelson Mandela did not face any problems, hardships or crises in their lives; they did, but they faced them with truth, fearlessness and compassion. They too had their fears but they had the courage to face up to their fears. That is the difference. They looked fear in the face and walked straight into it. They did not run away from a bad situation and neither did they blame somebody else for it. They understood and acted on the truth that life is not about being better than somebody else; life is about being a better person today than you were yesterday.

The challenge is, can I bring love, truth, peace and all such higher energy levels to bear upon my problems and try to find a solution through them? For instance, we may hate someone or something and we think that by overcoming hate for that one person or one particular thing, we have solved the problem. But that is not so, because tomorrow we may develop hatred for someone or something else. Until we realise that the problem is hatred itself and not who or what we hate, and we do not weed hatred out of our minds and hearts, we cannot solve the problems associated with hate. Until we collectively learn how to respond to each other's hatred with love, which is what Jesus, Buddha, Prophet Muhammad and all great spiritual masters taught us, responding to a negative force with more force will only create more problems.

Ultimately, I think that this is what each one of us is here to learn. We have to learn to identify the negative thoughts inside us and work towards removing such cancerous cells of negativity and defeatist thinking. If individually, each one of us can do this, then collectively, we would be able to overcome many of the problems we face as a society and will see dramatic improvement around us. The purpose of this book is to share individual problems and their possible solutions with potential readers to build a powerful, collective higher energy.

This book has thirty-two questions. Even if you fully read just five questions and their answers, and ask yourself, 'what did I learn', the 'light' will reach your inner space. As darkness cannot drive out darkness, only light can do that; as isolation cannot drive out ignorance, only knowledge can do that; similarly this process of learning, of letting the 'light' through will expand your mind, enrich your thoughts and refine your actions.

−APJ Abdul Kalam

Preparing
for success

Believe in yourself

Q Sir, I have always been lacking in confidence. In fact, both my brother and I are the same in this respect. Whether this is because of my mother who, when we were young, was over-protective and always shielded us from the realities of life, I am not sure. But now the problem has reached a point where it is affecting my day-to-day life. I feel that people around me must like me, even though I know that they actually don't. I had a friend at work, and I know it sounds crazy, but I felt that she would have lunch with me only because she felt sorry for me. If I need to go out of the house and some of my neighbours are outside, I wait for them to leave so that I do not have to confront them. The worst thing is that now I feel worthless. I find very little joy in my world. My tolerance for frustration has really gone down. I give up easily and wait for somebody else to take over the situation. Even temporary setbacks appear as permanent, intolerable conditions and I am always overcome by a sense of pessimism and hopelessness.

Yesterday I heard your speech where you said, "Believe in yourself! Have faith in your abilities! Without a humble but reasonable confidence in your own powers, you cannot be successful or happy." I know the reason for my unhappiness and lack of success. But how do I believe in myself? I have no grounds to raise my belief upon. I am sorry to say, but I do not see any abilities that I can count upon. I am confused. I am sure that what you are saying is the truth, but maybe in my case it does not apply. Please guide me - what should I do?

We gain strength, courage and confidence by each experience in which we really stop to look fear in the face. We must do that which we think we cannot
– Eleanor Roosevelt

My friend, it is clear that you need to build your self-confidence.

From the quietly confident doctor whose advice we rely on, to the charismatic confidence of an inspiring speaker, self-confident people have qualities that everyone admires. Self-confidence is indeed important in almost every aspect of our lives, yet so many people struggle to find it. Sadly, for you, this has become a vicious circle: because of your lack of self-confidence you are finding it difficult to become successful, and because you are not achieving success you are losing whatever self-confidence you have.

You will notice that in any sphere of life, people are reluctant to back a project that is being pitched by someone who is nervous, fumbling and overly apologetic. On the other hand, someone who speaks clearly, who holds his or her head high, who answers questions assuredly, and who readily admits when he or she does not know something, is able to gain your confidence.

Self-confident people inspire confidence in others, whether it be their audience, their peers, their bosses, their customers or their friends. And gaining the confidence of others is one of the key ways in which a self-confident person finds success. The good thing is that self-confidence can be learned and built upon. And, whether you are working

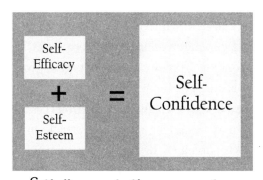

Self-efficacy and self-esteem contribute to self-confidence

on your own self-confidence or building the confidence of people around you, it is well worth the effort. So you need to work, and work hard to build your self-confidence.

The two main things which contribute to self-confidence are: self-efficacy and self-esteem. We gain a sense of self-efficacy when we see ourselves mastering skills and achieving goals in the skill areas which are important to us. This is the confidence that comes from knowing that if we work hard to build our expertise in a particular area, we will be to able succeed. And it is this type of confidence that leads people to accept difficult challenges and persist in the face of setbacks.

This overlaps with the idea of self-esteem, which is a general sense of knowing that we can cope with what's going on in our lives, and that we have a right to be happy. It also comes from knowing that we are behaving virtuously, that we are competent at what we do, and that we can compete successfully when we put our minds to it. Partly, this comes from a feeling that the people around approve of us.

In 1957 during my final academic year at the Madras Institute of Technology, while working on a group project, I learnt a very valuable lesson on how to create a sense of urgency for completing a given task in the assigned time. My teacher Prof Srinivasan formed a six-member team, with me as the project leader, for evolving a preliminary design for a low-level attack-aircraft and gave us six months to submit the design. I was responsible for the aerodynamic and structural design of the project. The other five members of our team took up the design of propulsion, control, guidance, avionics and instrumentation of the aircraft. After five months, when Prof Srinivasan reviewed the project he found our progress to be unsatisfactory and expressed his deep disappointment. He did not lend an ear to my long list of difficulties in bringing together databases from multiple designers. As I had to get inputs from five of my colleagues, without which I could not complete the system design, I asked for an additional month's time to complete the task. Prof Srinivasan said, "Look, young man, today is Friday afternoon.

I give you three days' time to show me the configuration design. If you can satisfy me, you will have an additional month. If not, your scholarship will be cancelled."

I got the biggest jolt of my life! The scholarship was my lifeline, without it I could not even pay for my food. There was no other way out but to finish the task in the assigned three days. My team members and I decided to give it our best. We worked round the clock, through the night, heads bent over the drawing board, skipping food and sleep. On Saturday, I took just an hour's break.

Self - Confidence

4 Work, work and work

3 Accelerate towards the goal

2 Set out to achieve the goal

1 Define your goal

Four steps to develop your self-confidence

On Sunday morning as I was working, I felt someone's presence in the laboratory. It was Prof Srinivasan, silently studying my progress. After looking at my work, he patted my back and hugged me affectionately and said, "I knew I was putting you under stress and asking you to meet a difficult deadline. But that was the only way to make you complete the project." Prof Srinivasan clearly set out the task for the next three days rather than allow us to grope in the dark for another month. The pressure of the deadline accelerated us towards the success that had been eluding us for the past few months. In the process of completing this project, I developed basic competence in my area of work and the soft skills needed to get cooperation from my team members.

What is the message this experience gives? That you can develop your self-confidence by following these four steps: one, define your goal, two, set out to achieve your goal, three, accelerate towards the goal and four, work, work and work.

Goal-setting is probably the most important activity that you can learn in order to improve your self-confidence. Set a goal for yourself in an area you love and work hard to achieve that goal. This will trigger a lifelong process of achieving success and you will also gain the confidence to successfully work with other people.

The power of dreams

Q Sir, motivated by your call to dream, I started to dream big. I imagined a world without limits where nothing could stand in my way. I never bothered to check any classified advertisements to see what jobs were available and nor did I care to understand whether my qualifications were relevant or not. I was going to be remarkable, I thought, and was filled with hope and expectations. Nothing could stop me. I believed that one day I would make it really big. And then something awful happened. It was not immediately obvious, in fact, I hardly noticed when it started to happen. It was subtle, but bit-by-bit it overcame me, and now it defines who I am. Without my really ever noticing or realising it, I gave up on my dreams. I became contented. I stopped hoping for more. Even worse, I stopped believing in something better. I gave in to the world around me and settled for what I am today. It's not that there is anything wrong with what I am today; it pays for my living, it keeps me safe, it keeps my life working. But once I tasted this giving in, this compromising, I decided to let it be my story. Why struggle? Why fight? Why be disappointed by unfulfilled dreams? There are no more obstacles in front of me because I 'dropped' out. No more difficulty. No more struggle. No more pain. Instead of pursuing my dreams, I decided to settle for something much less. But deep down inside me, I know that it does not have to be this way. Tell me, Dr Kalam, can I start dreaming again?

To succeed in life and achieve results, you must understand and master three mighty forces - desire, belief, and expectation
– APJ Abdul Kalam

Dreams are not those which you see in your sleep, dreams are those which don't let you sleep. But to make your dreams come true you have to be wide awake.

There is more opportunity today than ever before in the entire history of mankind. The twenty-first century is creating experiences thought to have been impossible in the last twenty centuries of human development. With technology and innovation driving humanity forward, the scope of human potential is increasing exponentially. However, the amount of time that we have to experience these opportunities is constant. And that is the dilemma the youth of today is facing. The youth want to, and should be able to, benefit from the widest range of experiences available to them, but as the world becomes more expansive, they are forced to keyhole themselves into narrower and more specialised domains. I do not think that is right. My dream is for every youth in the world to be able to experience as much of the world as they desire. But how is that possible?

There are two ways to make this possible. One, is to increase the amount of time that we have at our disposal. Another, is to increase the amount that we can do and achieve in the available time. Longevity and cognitive augmentation are the two life-goals I would like to present to every youth.

Understanding how to achieve these two life-goals will open the gates to everything else. This is the leap humanity has been waiting for and which will take us to the next stage in our evolution. So how do we do it? I give you two suggestions.

> *The two most important life-goals I would like every youth to have: one, increase the amount of time that you have at your disposal two, increase what you can achieve in the time available*

First, live a simple and pious life as it will help you remain healthy even as you grow old. This will make more time available to you to experience all that you would like to. With the passage of years, there is physical ageing and many 'age-related' diseases such as Alzheimer's, Parkinson's, cancer, heart-disorders start showing up. The important thing to understand is that each of these diseases takes decades to manifest themselves and very often their seeds are sown in young age. So now is the time to begin a wellness movement. Every youth must eat healthy, live healthy and think healthy. Your life is God's gift and no wealth of earth can ever match it, so why wither it away in addictions and bad habits? Maintain good health, keep away from bad habits, acquire the best education and skills. There are innumerable opportunities waiting for the worthy and competent, so forge ahead and avail of them.

Second, take responsibility for your life. Start by taking care of your parents. In Islam, one of the highest priorities after belief in God, is the love and care for parents. Prophet Muhammad said, 'Paradise is at the feet of the mother'. This is variously interpreted to mean that the mother is responsible for teaching her children their religious obligations and good behaviour that will earn them their place in paradise; or it may mean that you earn a place in paradise by serving your mother all through her life. Either way, it shows the great esteem, honour and respect that religion has for mothers. Once you arise and awake to assume responsibility towards your own life and your parents, the whole universe will work in your favour. There should be no doubt about this simple but profound truth.

The two essential wheels needed to roll over opportunities in life

But, simply having more time and taking responsibility for your life, by themselves, are not sufficient. To take advantage of the boundless new opportunities and possibilities that are available today, you need two other things, faith and determination. Faith and determination are the two essential wheels needed to roll over the opportunities in life. Without them the real meaning of life can never be realised. It is only our faith that keeps us committed to pursuing our goals with all our vigour even though we can never be sure of the outcome of our efforts. Determination is the power that sees us through all our frustrations and obstacles. It helps in building our will-power which is the very basis of success. It is said in the scriptures and Vedas that with the help of the power of determination, everything is possible. When the power of determination is not interrupted, one inevitably attains the desired goal.

Decide that no matter what happens, you will do what you set out to do. If you are determined, despite all the distractions that you may face, you will be able to continue on your chosen path and remain focused. It is not easy to change the circumstances of your life or the world to suit your requirements. But if you have the strength and determination, you can successfully face the challenges of life and in the process, sometimes you may even be able to change the world itself.

Determination is the power that sees us through all our frustrations and obstacles It helps in building our willpower which is the very basis of success

Patience is another great virtue that needs to be cultivated. One should always pay attention to one's determination, sincere efforts, patience, regularity and loving nature. Always try to be vigilant, so that negative forces do not take over. Whenever you find an obstacle, you should learn to be patient. You will have to practise patience when you start plumbing the depths of your mind. If you persist, finally, you will find the light that dispels the darkness of ignorance. The time will come when you will know all that is to be known. Do not allow the gentle and eternal flame, which burns within each of us, to die out.

> *Never give up*
> *on your dreams*
> *no matter how*
> *old you are*
> *no matter where*
> *you are today*
> *Do not give up*
> *dreaming for a*
> *better tomorrow*

My answer to your question, 'Can I start dreaming again?', is, be optimistic and tenacious when facing adversities. Never give up on your dreams, no matter how old you are or where you are today. Do not ever give up dreaming for a better tomorrow. Remain steadfast in your faith, refine your professional skills, embrace innovation, work hard and build noble character. The most exhilarating experiences of my life have emerged out of my dreams and sincere expectations. If, with all your heart, you seize the opportunities that come your way, you will experience great accomplishments.

Navigating time

Q Sir, I often find myself being overwhelmed by the sheer number and complexity of tasks that I need to complete at work each day. In the morning I list out all the tasks that I have to accomplish during the day. But as the day goes by, I start feeling that I have not paid enough attention to each task because other tasks kept landing on my desk or co-workers kept interrupting me with questions. I just cannot seem to get myself organised. I have tried following a timetable but I get frustrated and give up because no matter what I plan, I am not able to follow it. Very often, I am not able to finish a task in the time that I had set aside for it, and then have to cut corners or stay up late to get it done at the last minute. And not having given the task the required time and attention it deserved, I know that it does not reflect the best that I am capable of.

Sir, you have managed many big national projects such as the SLV3, missiles, the nuclear bomb and delivered them on time. What is the secret of your time management?

The future is something, which everyone reaches at the rate of sixty minutes an hour, whatever he or she does, whoever the person is
– C S Lewis

Time is said to be eternal. It is said that time has neither a beginning nor an end. Yet human beings are able to measure and define time as years, months, days, hours, minutes and seconds. They have been able to give meaning to the words - past, present and future. Time never stops, it keeps moving. What was yesterday is not today. What is today will not be tomorrow. Yesterday is gone. Tomorrow is yet to come. Today is here and using today wisely is the key to success.

As you all know, the earth rotates on its own axis once in 24 hours or 1440 minutes or 86400 seconds, causing day and night. The earth orbits around the sun taking nearly one year to complete an orbit. With the completion of one orbit of the earth around the sun, your age increases by one year. Every movement of creation is linked with time. There is birth,

If you waste time

Time wastes you

Time never stops

growth and death. A child is born, grows into adolescence, youth, middle age and old age with the passage of time. Seasons come according to time. Plants flower and give fruits. One cannot grow paddy in a month nor can a child become an adult in a year. There is a time for everything and everything happens according to its time.

Time is a free force. It does not wait for anyone. It is commonly said that time and tide wait for no man. Time is money. A minute not usefully spent is an eternal loss. You can never get back that lost minute. One has to strike the iron when it is hot because time gone by never returns. If you waste time, it wastes you. Shakespeare has expressed it so eloquently in *Julius Caesar* (act 4, scene 3):

> 'There is a tide in the affairs of men
> Which, taken at the flood, leads on to fortune
> Omitted, all the voyage of their life
> Is bound in shallows and in miseries
> On such a full sea are we now afloat
> And we must take the current when it serves
> Or lose our ventures'

'Time is the best medicine', wrote the Roman poet Ovid (43 BC - AD 18). It is said that time heals all wounds including those which reason cannot. All human beings are emotional and when negative emotions like fear, anger, envy and jealousy overtake us, we lose reason and act in haste leading to serious consequences. Later, as emotions cool down we may repent our actions. But the damage is done and remains forever. However, with the passage of time that damage can heal. The people involved may forget and forgive. That is the importance of time and its healing touch.

Time is also said to be a wise counsellor. The passage of time allows an individual to grow. This growth provides experience which helps in decision-making. Time reminds you to act, and act wisely. Some people merely keep thinking about how to spend their time while the wise and talented make use of their time fruitfully. It is said that the wisest grieve the most at the loss of time.

There is a proverb
which says that
killing time is
not murder but
suicide
By wasting time
one is not harming others
but oneself

Those who do not know the importance of time, waste it or rather they spend it doing nothing. There is a proverb, which says that killing time is not murder, it is suicide. It means that by wasting time one is not harming others but harming himself or herself.

Some people always complain that there is not enough time for them to do everything. That is not correct. If one wisely plans his or her activities, there will be time for everything. Man, who is a part of nature, cannot complain against time. Man has only to obey it. Time is powerful, it conquers all. Every day, every person gets the same twenty-four hours to use as he or she likes. Out of those twenty-four hours, time which is available to a person to use the way he or she likes is most valuable. I learnt this early in my life and started purposefully navigating my time rather than flowing with its perpetual routines. If you are not on time and miss

Time is the
key to success
We have no
control over it
The only thing
that we can do
is navigate it

a train, you miss it forever. So also with time, once you miss it or waste it, it is gone forever. You can never catch it or get it back. That is why it is called fleeting time.

Time is the key to success. We have no control over it. The only thing that we can do is learn to navigate time to reach our goal or destination. Let us learn to use our time fruitfully. Let not thy winged days be spent in vain.

Overcoming failures

Q I have reached this point in my life where I feel I have totally failed. I was a good student in school and scored reasonable marks in my 10th class and got admission in a Government college for a Diploma in Electronics. But I was not really interested in the subject and the lecturers were not good at teaching. The final examination is over and I have failed in one subject. Now I have to wait for one long year to re-write this examination. Though my parents are calm, I do not have the strength to face my friends and relatives. I often have this strong feeling that life is not worth living, and I have even attempted to slash my wrists and end my life.

In the 12th class examination, I got an average of 70.8 per cent in five subjects, and 58 per cent in physics, chemistry and mathematics. In the Bangalore joint examination I got the 35,000th rank, which I know will get me admission only into a mediocre college, for an engineering course, not of my choice. My parents have no hope from me and my father says, "I am wasting all my money on you in vain... you are such a thickhead and I'm ashamed to be your father." Tell me Sir, am I a failure?

Every adversity, every failure, every heartache carries with it the seed of an equal or greater solution
– Napolean Hill

Dear friend, there is no success without failure. Success is the final destination. Failures are intermittent blockades. If you cross the blockades with courage and conviction, you will overcome the failures and attain success in your life.

Let me tell you the story of Srinivasa Ramanujan who is hailed as one of the world's greatest mathematicians. In a short life of mere thirty-two years, and with little formal training, he made extraordinary contributions to mathematical analysis, number theory, infinite series, and continued fractions and left behind 4000 original theorems. Born in 1887 in Erode in Tamil Nadu, Ramanujan, even as a child demonstrated a natural ability for mathematics. By the age of twelve Ramanujan had

There is no success without failure Failures are just intermittent blockades Success is the final destination

discovered theorems of his own. Living and working in India, with no access to the larger mathematical community which was centred in Europe at the time, Ramanujan developed his own mathematical research. And by the time he turned seventeen,

Srinivasa Ramanujan

Ramanujan had conducted his own research on Bernoulli numbers and the Euler-Mascheroni constant.

Ramanujan received a scholarship to study at the Government College in Kumbakonam, but was withdrawn when he failed his non-mathematical coursework. He joined another college to pursue independent mathematical research and also started working as a clerk in the Accountant-General's office at the Madras Port Trust Office to support himself. In January 1912, Ramanujan sent some of his work to Prof G H Hardy at Trinity College in Cambridge University in England, who was considered to be one of the most brilliant mathematicians at the time. Prof Hardy recognised the genius of Ramnujan's work and invited him to work at Cambridge. Ramanujan later became a Fellow of the Royal Society and a Fellow of Trinity College, Cambridge. He spent five years at Cambridge where he published 21 papers. Unfortunately he was plagued by health problems throughout his life. Living in a country far away from home, and obsessively involved with mathematics, Ramanujan's health worsened, perhaps exacerbated by stress and the scarcity of vegetarian food. In 1919, he fell seriously ill with tuberculosis, and returned to India. He died soon thereafter, at the young age of thirty-two.

What all hardships did Ramanujan not suffer? But these hardships did not deter his genius. Though suffering and hardship seem to be destructive and negative, but in the long term, these may sometimes be balanced or even transcended by powerful, positive after-effects.

The German philosopher, Friedrich Nietzsche, too suffered immensely. For most of his life, he endured excruciating migraines which left him incapacitated for days, as well as terrible stomach pains. He was forced to retire from his professorship at University of Basel in Switzerland at the age of thirty-five due to his ill health, and spend the rest of his life in isolation. He had very few friends, never found a wife or girlfriend, and was ostracized by his own intellectual peers because of his unconventional ideas. He was so unsuccessful as an author that he had to pay for his books to be published, and later many of them even

Friedrich Nietzsche

had to be pulped because there were no buyers for them! By the time his writings eventually began to filter through to appreciative readers, he was showing signs of mental instability. At the age of forty-five he had a complete mental breakdown and spent the last ten years of his life in a catatonic state.

Nietszche had remarkable powers of resilience and always thought that his suffering was beneficial to him. He saw his suffering as 'the ultimate emancipator of spirit' which was essential for his philosophy, since it, 'forces us philosophers to descend into our nethermost depths...I doubt whether such suffering improves a man; but I know that it makes him deeper'. His experience was that when a person emerges from episodes of illness, isolation or humiliation, he is 'as though born again, he has a new skin', with a 'finer taste for joyfulness'. In his book, *The Prophet*, Kahlil Gibran makes a similar point when he writes that, 'The deeper that sorrow carves into your being, the more joy you can contain.'

I am not saying that we should welcome suffering or purposely seek it out. But when it does appear in our lives, we should be aware that, beneath its negative surface, there could be a hidden opportunity for growth and deepening. None of us is a failure.

Is it not a miracle that we exist, that we are alive, that we are healthy, can think, go around places, and do so many things?

When suffering appears in our lives we should be aware that beneath its negative surface there could be a hidden opportunity for growth and deepening

Steve Taylor in his book, *Out of the Darkness: From Turmoil to Transformation*, shares amazing stories of enlightenment brought about by life's most difficult circumstances. It helps us to realise that we can always choose to make something good out of the worst that life sometimes brings for us, thereby greatly reducing our fears and inviting happiness to embrace us. Therefore, never consider yourself a failure. I can only say that psychological turmoil can be the catalyst for a kind of 'spiritual alchemy', transforming the 'base metal' of suffering into the 'gold' of intense well-being and freedom. In a spiritual sense, turmoil has some sort of an 'awakening' effect, and illustrates the almost

> *Use the difficult situation*
> *you are facing to*
> *tap into your spirituality*
> *and build upon it to*
> *achieve something meaningful*

infinite capacity of human beings to overcome suffering. That is the reason why some people emerge from difficult times and situations stronger, wiser and more grateful, while others sink into depression, bitterness or resignation.

So long as we have the courage to face up to, and accept negative situations, there is nothing to fear. But perhaps most importantly, it shows how natural is spiritual awakening to human beings, and how close it is to all of us. Use the difficult situation you are facing, to tap into your spirituality and build upon it, to achieve something meaningful in your life.

Attributes of courage

Q Sir, I heard your speech on courage. Courage is a quality we all want to imbibe. It is indeed an attribute of good character that makes us worthy of respect. From the scriptures to fairy tales, from ancient myths to movies, there are exemplary tales of courage and self-sacrifice. From the young boy in the film, *The Life of Pi*, who finds the courage to co-exist with a tiger aboard his boat in the middle of the Atlantic Ocean, to David battling Goliath in the Bible, to Prahlada fearlessly sitting on a pyre, and the Harry Potter stories, we have been raised on a diet of heroic and inspirational tales. History books tell us about courageous people, such as Mahatma Gandhi and Nelson Mandela, who chose to speak out against injustice at great personal risk; entrepreneurs such as Steve Jobs and Walt Disney who took business risks to innovate and follow their dreams. All of them are like modern-day knights, exemplifying the rewards and public accolades that courage can bring.

But, Sir, we hardly see any courage in our leaders. Terrorists who have killed thousands of our fellow citizens are openly living abroad without any fear of the law. Similarly, no action is taken against people who are looting our nationalised banks by taking huge loans for spurious ventures but using them instead for their personal gains, and not repaying the banks. There are people who have parked their ill-gotten money in foreign banks, and people who do not pay taxes, but no action is taken against them. Why are we so helpless as a nation? Why are we lacking in courage to take the right steps? Where is the courage?

Faced with what is right, to leave it undone shows a lack of courage
– Confucius

You have asked a very important question. While we are all familiar with the historical and mythical stories of the lives of courageous people, but it seems that in real life not many people are able to live and act courageously. I consider this weakness to be at the root of most of our social evils. There is so much widespread gender bias, social inequality, unacceptable income differences, lack of efficiency and duty-consciousness, and yet people do not stand up against the wrongs being done. I will not load you with any theoretical answers but will share with you, the practical attributes of courage that I have observed in my own dealings with situations.

The first and most important attribute of courage is choosing to act despite experiencing fear. Fear and courage are indeed two sides of the same coin. Courage is not the absence of fear, but the triumph over it. A brave person is not one who is afraid of his fear, but who conquers that fear. There is no living being that is not afraid when it faces danger. True courage is in facing danger when you are afraid. Courage is about doing what you are afraid to do. The one who feels no fear is a fool and the one who lets fear rule him is indeed a coward. We must have the courage to act instead of reacting.

> *Courage is about doing what you are afraid to do The one who feels no fear is a fool and the one who lets fear rule him is indeed a coward We must have the courage to act instead of reacting*

Since childhood, I had nurtured a dream to fly. That was the reason I studied Aeronautical Engineering. After completing my course, I applied for a short-service commission in the Indian Air Force. But I was rejected in the interview and a dream cherished over the years was shattered in an instant. I trekked up to Rishikesh in the Himalayas and spent some time there, trying to come to terms with what had happened. Later, I joined Hindustan Aeronautics Limited as a maintenance engineer. Many of us give up on life when we don't get what we have been aspiring for, be it a job, a relationship or anything else. Courage is the ability to be able to cope with the disappointment of not getting what we desire, and yet, move on in life.

Attributes of courage

> Experiencing fear and yet choosing to act
> Following your heart
> Persevering in the face of adversity
> Standing up for what is right
> Expanding your horizons and letting go of the familiar
> Facing suffering with dignity and faith

The second attribute of courage is to follow your heart. Passion is what drives our creativity, what makes us do extraordinary things, what makes us discover and challenge ourselves. Passion is at the heart of courage. When you follow your heart and intuition, you realise that you already know what you truly want to become. Everything else is secondary. In choosing to dare you may momentarily lose your footing but to not dare is to risk losing your own self.

In 2006, as the President of India, I held on for eighteen days before signing The Office of Profit Bill. I was not at peace with the collective convenience of self-interest being sought to be served by our political leaders. The options were to block the Bill once and then append my signature or exercise inordinate delay or resign and create political instability which I didn't want to do. After several rounds of self-questioning and introspection, I returned the Bill to the Parliament for reconsideration. The Bill was again sent to me for my assent. Once I received the confirmation that the Parliament had constituted a Joint Parliamentary Committee (JPC) to go into all the aspects of The Office of Profit Bill as per my suggestions, I finally signed the

Bill in order to uphold the convention. I realised that if the majority party in the Lok Sabha is bent on passing a law which is against the spirit of the Constitution or which is in their own favour, it becomes very difficult for the President to discharge his responsibility. Realising this limitation, I made the conscious decision that I would not opt for a second term of office, but would rather spend my time trying to ignite the minds of the people and the youth towards the India Vision 2020. It takes courage to endure the sharp pains of self-discovery rather than choose the dull pain of a knowing consciousness that would last the rest of your life.

Most of our obstacles melt away if instead of cowering before them we make up our mind to walk boldly through them

The third attribute of courage is persevering in the face of adversity. When we are feeling afraid or when faced with danger, we should not try to convince ourselves that there is no danger, but rather spend our time and energy in strengthening ourselves to go on in spite of the danger. When I was a child living in Rameswaram, I remember there was once a huge cyclone and my father lost his boat. The boat was used for ferrying passengers and without the boat my father had no means of earning money to meet the expenses for the survival of our large extended family. At that time, we were ruled by the British and there was no concept of government relief for such natural disasters. There was no one who was willing to give a loan to my father. So my father decided to build a new boat. Day after day, watching him toil over building the new boat, I learnt that most of our obstacles melt away if, instead of cowering before them, we make up our minds to walk boldly through them. I learnt from my father that 'courage is not the roaring proclamation of victory', it is the little voice at the end of the day that says, tomorrow I shall try again. "Give up my boat?" my father would have thought, "Not at all! Sell the wood wreckage and do something else? Impossible!" So he put in long weeks of hard, physical labour and rebuilt his boat all by himself.

In choosing to dare you may momentarily lose your footing but to not dare is to risk losing yourself

In 1973, I was appointed as the Project Director of India's first Satellite Launch Vehicle (SLV). My team and I worked for six long years to build it. On August 10, 1979 when it was finally launched, instead of launching the satellite into orbit, the rocket fell into the Bay of Bengal. Years of hard work and effort had come to a nought! But the disaster did not deter us from making corrections and finally, on July 18, 1980 we successfully launched the Rohini satellite into orbit. Temporary setbacks should be viewed as stepping stones for course correction and not as insurmountable obstacles which should make you change your goals.

Courage is standing up for what is right

The fourth attribute of courage is standing up for what is right. Courageous people stand up for something because they believe it is the right thing to do, not because they believe that it will save their lives. Such selfless courage is victory in itself. In the 1960s, I was working as a rocket engineer in Thiruvananthapuram in the Space Science and Technology Centre, now known as the Vikram Sarabhai Space Centre. We were developing a sodium vapour payload for use in sounding rockets which could go up to 150 kilometres. Sodium payload is prepared using multiple layers of dry sodium and thermite, in alternate layers, in a steel chamber of 200 millimetre diameter and 500 millimetre length. Each layer is pressed with a 500 tonne

The world demands the qualities of youth, youth not as defined by a time span of life but defined by a state of mind a temper of the will a quality of the imagination a predominance of courage over timidity and an appetite for adventure over a life of ease

hydraulic press. We had prepared nearly ten sodium payloads. These sodium payloads were to be launched with the sounding rockets, to explore the atmospheric wind conditions, by monitoring the sodium vapour cloud released at 60 kilometre altitude.

The preparation of the eleventh payload was under way in the sodium payload laboratory in a specially sealed filling room in which the temperature was maintained at 25 degree celsius and humidity at 10 per cent. When the payload process started and half the chamber was filled, there was a power breakdown for few seconds before the stand-by generator was switched on. At that time, I was with my team member, V Sudhakar. As things were

Only the person who has the courage to lose sight of the shore can discover new oceans

moving smoothly and only fifteen minutes of the filling operation remained, I decided to return to the control room of the laboratory. Just as I stepped out of the sealed filling room, I heard a loud explosion. As I looked back towards the room I could see flames! For the first time we were all witness to the ferocity of a sodium fire. Because the sodium was in a sealed room, the only way to escape the fire was through the glass window of the room. Sudhakar smashed open the glass window and pushed out the three colleagues working with him and then jumped out after them. Sudhakar did what was necessary for saving the lives of his colleagues without any thought for his own safety.

The fifth attribute of courage is expanding your horizons and letting go of the familiar. Only the person who has the courage to lose sight of the shore can discover new oceans. This world demands the qualities of youth; youth not as defined by a time-span of life but by a state of mind, a temper of the will, a quality of the imagination, a predominance of courage over timidity, of an appetite for adventure over a life of ease. Life shrinks or expands in proportion to one's courage. If I had not left the safety of home at Rameswaram and gone to Tiruchirapalli for my college education, and on to Chennai to study engineering, and then left Tamil Nadu to work in Uttar Pradesh, Karnataka and Kerala, my story would not have turned out as it has and I would not be sharing it with you today.

Courage is the most important of all the virtues because without courage you cannot practise any other virtue consistently

Lastly, courage is facing suffering with dignity and faith. A person of

Nelson Mandela

courage is a person full of faith. A courageous person bears the accidents of life with dignity and grace, making the best of his circumstances. Courage is the most important of all the virtues because without courage you cannot practise any other virtue consistently. You can practise any virtue erratically, but nothing consistently without courage. I once asked my friend Nelson Mandela, "What kept you going during the twenty-seven long years you spent in prison?" He said, "Kalam, I learnt that courage is not the absence of fear, but the triumph over it. A brave man is not he who does not feel afraid, but he who conquers his fear."

Coming to your question, Where is the courage? Courage is in your heart, it is in your character. As a nation, it is essential for us to elect the right type of leaders and stand up against wrongdoings and injustices that we see around us. Courage is to dream for a better life even in the most difficult times and to awaken to your potential even in the most hopeless situation.

Indomitable spirit

Q We are living in a time when countless new problems keep cropping up everyday. If we are to solve these problems, we need leaders who have the courage to think bold new ideas and the courage to endure criticism of these new ideas. Sadly, good people in our country, be they teachers, philosophers, spiritual leaders, artists and intellectuals, all confine themselves within the safety of their own small worlds. Even if they have a bold and new idea, they are afraid of expressing it because of the scorn and ridicule they may receive from others. They fear what others may think of their ideas.

But, Sir, you are different. You stood up for your ethics and principles, even when it was not convenient, and even when it was to your detriment. The second Presidential term was yours for the taking but you declined it because of the conditions that came attached with it. What message do you have for countless people like me, cold and timid souls, who know neither victory nor defeat?

No one is less ready for tomorrow than the person who holds the most rigid beliefs about what tomorrow will bring
— Watts Wacker, Jim Taylor and Howard Means

I did not accept the offer of the second Presidential term because I was not willing to get into any kind of political alignments and wranglings while sitting as the eleventh President of India. It is my belief that for the highest position in the country, both the ruling party and the opposition need to come together to unanimously elect the President. Though contest and election cannot be avoided in a democracy, but by and large, there should be unanimity while electing the President, because I believe it is the repository of the confidence of the people in the highest office of the country. I did not want to create any instability in the political atmosphere and so I chose not to accept the offer of a second term, and instead decided to devote my energy towards realising the India Vision 2020.

Your mail indeed conveys a very common problem, that of our disconnect from the spirit that resides inside each one of us. We do not exercise the power of our spirit because we lack an understanding of its character and its relation to our mind. We need to understand that everything originates from the human mind, and the power of the mind originates from our spirit. From our spirit we can derive power not only over our mind, but over almost any idea or thought in the world. I call this power, the Indomitable Spirit.

The body of Indomitable Spirit stands on two feet; one, of vision for higher goals and two, firm thought.

In order to connect with your spirit you must have a vision for your life. To define the vision for your life, you need to do serious soul searching. As Carl Jung said, "Your vision will become clear only when you look into your heart. Who looks outside, finds a dream; who looks inside, awakens." Strangely most of us shy away from the use of vision, perhaps because we equate having a vision with being impractical. My contention, however, is that vision is intensely practical, and that while it should reflect our values and aspirations, it must be based on facts.

Vision

Firm Thought

Vision has two components. It is part emotional (the product of our imagination, intuition, and values) and part rational (the product of analysis).

The body of Indomitable Spirit stands on two feet

I use the term vision in a very precise and detailed sense. Without this precision, vision can drift off into the realms of fantasy and lack the practical power, which if better defined, it should possess. Vision is the ability to perceive something which is not physically visible, but is visible only through mental acuteness and keen foresight. When I call upon youth to dream lofty dreams, I am invoking a vision in them. As you dream, so shall you become! Your vision is the promise of what, one day, you shall be. Your ideal is the prophecy of what you shall unveil at last. It is the vision which provides direction and purpose to your life. When you don't have a vision, you don't know what you are working towards or even what you are living for. You are like a ship that has been put out on the high seas without a captain or a destination. The ship is at the mercy of the waves which can toss it around anywhere and everywhere. But once you have a vision, you then have a defined destination, or at least a direction, and you can steer the ship of your life in that direction. Dissatisfaction and discouragement are not caused so much by the absence of things as by the absence of vision.

> *When I call upon youth to dream lofty dreams I am invoking a vision in them As you dream so shall you become!*

Firm thought is the second component of indomitable spirit. There is this concept of *stithpragya* described in *Bhagvadgita* (chapter 2, verse 68) which explains the key to success in this manner: 'The person who has control over his senses, his mind is stable and his inner self is calm.' To achieve any kind of success you first have to succeed in controlling your

> *To achieve any success you have to first control your sense and when this is combined with vision you can achieve any goal*

senses. Having mastered that, and combined with your vision, you can achieve any goal that you choose.

Two thousand years ago, the poet-saint Thiruvalluvar wrote in *Kural* (verse 595): 'With rising flood the lotus flower stem unwinds, the dignity of men is measured by their minds.' This means that just as the length of the lotus stem is proportionate to the depth of the water; so is men's greatness proportionate to their minds. If there is a definite determination to achieve a goal, no matter how difficult it is, you will succeed.

In my life I have been responsible for managing several large programmes and projects. Many times I experienced difficult situations when success was nowhere in sight and there were many hurdles; hurdles created by man, hurdles created by the nature of the programme or hurdles created by technology.

Mental strength is the most powerful source of support when we are going through difficult times If we delve into the deep depths of our being we can find the inner strength to keep moving towards our goal no matter how difficult the path may seem

There were enough reasons for me to get discouraged and give up, but I did not. As saint Thiruvalluvar in *Kural* (verse 622) says: 'Deluging sorrows come to nought, when wise men face them with firm thought.' This explains that mental strength is the most powerful source of support to a person going through difficult times. If we delve into the deep depths of our being, we can find that inner strength to keep moving towards our goal no matter how difficult the path may seem.

In 2004, while flying to the Car Nicobar island to see the tsunami affected areas, I wrote this poem, "Indomitable Spirit":

I was swimming in the sea
Waves came one after the other
I was swimming and swimming to reach my destination
But one wave, a powerful wave, overpowered me
It took me along in its own direction
I was pulled long and along
When I was about to lose amidst the sea wave power
One thought flashed to me, yes, that is courage
Courage to reach my goal
Courage to defeat the powerful force and succeed;
With courage in my mind, indomitable spirit engulfed me
With indomitable spirit in mind and action
I regained lost confidence
I can win, win and win
Strength came back to me, overpowered the sea wave
I reached the destination, my mission

Qualities of
an unstoppable person

Q Sir, I read your book, *Squaring the Circle: Seven Steps to Indian Renaissance.* The idea of an Indian renaissance is both interesting and inspiring. As my friends and I could not make any sense of the title of the book, we asked our teachers about it. The mathematics teacher said that squaring the circle is impossible as it would require constructing the length $\sqrt{\pi}$ as the area of a circle with radius r is πr^2. Hence a square with the same area must have a side of r $\sqrt{\pi}$. And this number cannot be constructed as π is not an exact number. There are no rational numbers that can calculate π and it is impossible to construct $\sqrt{\pi}$ in Euclidean space. The English teacher said that, 'squaring the circle' is an idiom which means to find a good solution to a problem that seems impossible, especially because the people involved have very different perceptions or opinions about it.

From both these answers I understand that you have used 'squaring the circle' as a metaphor for trying to do the impossible. So is an Indian renaissance impossible to usher? Or are you trying to get the two sets of our politicians, ruling and opposition, to agree to 'square the circle' for the task of developing our country. Please clarify.

Who looks outside, dreams. Who looks inside, awakens
– Carl Gustav Jung

When I am talking of renaissance, I mean people who succeed in life with commitment (to their vision), perseverance (in spite of fear) and confidence (belief in themselves). After more than six decades of independence, we as a nation still seem to be moving in circles. Though a certain level of development has taken place and much wealth has been generated, the lives of the majority of Indians are yet to experience any significant improvement. We need to square up our act and move decisively so as to achieve our goal of a developed and peaceful nation.

A nation is built up of families and the individual members who form the families. There is a cascade from individual to nation that works both ways, in a vicious circle and in a virtuous circle, a complex chain of events that reinforces itself through a feedback loop. These circles or cycles continue in the direction of their momentum until an external factor intervenes and breaks the cycle. How can the vicious cycle, that we are currently in, be broken?

Who will break it? My book seeks answers to these two questions, but since you have read the book, I will not discuss it here. Instead, I will share with you my idea of an unstoppable person. There are six qualities which an unstoppable person possesses.

Once we commit to a goal there is a mental shift from thought to action and instantly we have a purpose and direction

The first quality is the ability to dream, commit and take action. We all have a passion, a dream or a goal. It may be to write a book, feed the hungry, plant trees, run a free dispensary, build a temple, a mosque or a community hall; whatever that dream or goal is, once we commit to it, there is a mental shift from thought to action. Instantly, we have a purpose and a direction. We no longer let circumstances run our life, instead we take the helm and steer our ship of life towards the desired destination or goal.

On the journey towards our destination, how we weather the storms that we encounter is proof of how true our commitment is. It is not enough to simply commit and then cave in to self-doubt, criticism, disappointment and frustration, which is sure to come up when we are trying to achieve anything worthwhile. If we are truly committed, then we need to have a pit bull like determination to achieve our goal. The key to success lies in making the achievement of that goal a priority in our life, above everything else, and even being ready to make sacrifices for it.

The second quality is having confidence and belief in yourself. If you truly think you can do something, then you can actually get it done, and if you think you cannot do it, you will not be able to do it. As Henry Ford rightly said, 'Whether you think you can or you think you can't, you're right.' Confidence in ourselves, and in what we are committed to, increases the chances of achieving our goal. The resolve that failure is not an option is the mentality that creates miracles.

The third quality is faith. Faith helps us focus on the final outcome. Having faith is an inner knowing or a belief, even in the absence of any evidence, that eventually things will work out. Faith is knowing deep down in our hearts that, if we keep focusing on the end result and consistently laying the groundwork to make it happen, then the desired final outcome will be achieved.

Happiness is not attained through self-gratification but through commitment to a worthy purpose If we devote ourselves to a purpose and combine it with passion our life becomes meaningful and we have a recipe for greatness

The fourth quality is the courage to succeed, no matter what. We must not let criticism get in the way of our goal. People can be harsh when they see other people moving outside of what is considered normal behaviour. They may feel threatened by a person's changed behaviour. But, if this interferes with our commitments, all is lost. It takes great courage to push past criticism and continually be true to who you are and what you want.

Fifth is overcoming obstacles by persevering. I am greatly inspired by the life of Abraham Lincoln. He failed many times and was severely criticised by his opponents, friends and even his own family. If he would have let the critcism affect him and given up on his dream, his extraordinary vision for his country would have been wasted. What the United States of America is today, is in a large measure because of the vision of Lincoln. This is the power of perseverance, the willingness to press on in spite of criticism, failure, fear, and self-doubt. We must have the mental toughness and inner strength to stay committed to our dream.

Qualities of an unstoppable person

> Dream, commit and take action
> Have confidence and belief in yourself
> Have faith
> Have the courage to succeed no matter what
> Overcome obstacles by perseverance
> Be purposeful & passionate

The sixth quality is purposefulness and passion. Many persons have the wrong idea about what constitutes true happiness. Happiness is not attained through self-gratification but through commitment to a worthy purpose. To be true to what we want, is an important act of self-love which gives purpose and meaning to our life. Once we devote ourselves to a worthy purpose, our life becomes meaningful, and when it is combined with passion, we have a recipe for greatness. We have to ensure that we do not get distracted from our goals by life's curve balls and our daily obligations, and continue steadfastly on our chosen path.

Inshallah

Q   Sir, every now and then I get this feeling that, even though I am spinning the wheel of my life, I am not reaching anywhere. I know I am doing my best, but it feels as though I am just mechanically going through the motions of life. I feel I am not doing what I was meant to do, I am not making any progress and have reached a plateau. It is a letdown, because I know deep down that I could be doing so much better. I always had this special feeling inside me that I was meant for greatness. It was this feeling that compelled me to continue even when I believed all was lost, that my moment had passed and there was no reason to continue striving. But I continued my efforts, not because someone told me to, but because I could not help it; and no matter how many times I quit, no matter how many times I gave up, something made me get back on my feet and try again.

But Sir, now this feeling scares me. I am getting convinced that I am not living up to my potential and each day that goes by is another day lost forever and I am not fulfilling my destiny. Is destiny not a dangerous belief? Is it not a mythical destination without any roadmap to get there?

Sir, you put India's first satellite in orbit, created five missile systems and helped build a nuclear bomb and its delivery system. Starting from a nondescript Rameswaram island you reached the majestic Rashtrapati Bhawan. What kept you going? Were you not scared? Did you know your destination? Did you pursue your success or did it just happen to you?

There are no 'ifs' in God's world. And no places that are safer than other places. The centre of His will is our only safety - let us pray that we may always know it
– Corrie ten Boom

My late friend R Swaminathan and I would sometimes discuss the issue of destiny versus free will that you have talked about in your question. Are we free agents of our own will or are we mere puppets in the hands of destiny? Can we change our fate? One view is that we are prisoners of fate and no matter what we do, we simply cannot change it. Another view is that we are absolutely free and have the freedom of choosing between right or wrong. You have asked, can destiny be altered by our actions and efforts? Your mail took me back to the discussions

I would have with Swaminathan. And through this mail to you, I will attempt to answer the question my friend left me with.

There are three types of powerful forces we all carry within us. The first force is that of our unexplained drives and impulses. The second force is that of our dispositions. Each one of us is inclined towards certain things, some are attracted to music, some to art, some to physical activity, some to mental activity, some others to spiritual pursuits and some are attracted towards scientific subjects. And the third force is our free will. At any moment, our actions are propelled by a combination of these three forces.

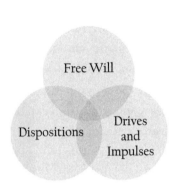

Three powerful forces that we carry within us

Let me illustrate with an example of the bow and arrow as used by an archer. The accumulated stock of arrows in the archer's case slung over his shoulder represents our drives and impulses. The arrow that the archer has just shot from his bow represents the archer's disposition and the arrow in his hand at the moment represents the archer's free will. He can decide not to use this arrow, or he can choose to use it either to protect the weak or to harass them. Thus, while disposition is something which cannot be changed or undone, but at all times we have our free will available to us to choose our actions.

But how do we know which are the forces that form part of our destiny? Is death, disease or wealth part of destiny? If everyone's date of death is pre-decided, what then is the role of medical science?

In his last days, Swaminathan was full of such questions. His questions made me realise that I was not equipped to help him understand the role of destiny versus free will. But now your mail has compelled me to sit down and attempt to complete this task.

All the three forces, our drives, dispositions and free will, play a role in every aspect of our life, including taking action in an extreme situation of trying to save someone from the jaws of death. At the time of action, one should not think of one's destiny, because no one can predict it. The drives and impulses theory is useful in explaining the action. But in spite of taking actions and our best efforts, if results are not achieved, it can be attributed to destiny. The theory of destiny is useful as it helps a person accept results without being frustrated. In the same way, if he understands the role of destiny in his success, it prevents a successful person from becoming egoistic.

Is it possible that even a person's free will, that is, his inclination to put in efforts to achieve something, is influenced by destiny? I turn to the scriptures for an answer. 'Yes, but rarely so', the scriptures inform me. The example of Rama deciding to go after the golden deer is given to explain the rare situation when the course of destiny that was to happen influenced his free will. 'Lauh al-Mahu w al-Ithbat', is an Arabic phrase which reflects the Muslim doctrine that Allah has measured out the span of every person's life, their lot of good or ill-fortune, and the fruits of their efforts. When referring to the future, Muslims frequently qualify any predictions of what will come to pass with the phrase 'Inshallah' which means 'God willing'.

Now the question arises if my drives and dispositions are 'given' what can I do with my free will? Is free will not 'given' to me? I would say that, free will and drives and dispositions, are like the twin blades of a pair of scissors. Only when the two blades act together, can the scissors do its job. Just as you cannot cut a piece of cloth with one blade of the scissors, likewise, both, drives and dispositions, and free will are necessary for action.

*Our free will and
drives and dispositions
are like the twin blades
of a pair of scissors
Only when the two
blades act together
can the scissors do its job
Both free will and disposition
are necessary for action*

Our drives and dispositions determine many things that we cannot change. For instance, we have no control over the type of family into which we are born, our race and the type of body which we have. I might wish to change the shape of my nose or increase my height by a few centimetres, and while technology is increasingly finding ways to do so, but for most of us, these are unchangeable realities. Also, the reality is that we all are not created equal. In the same family, all the children do not have equal ability or intelligence. Is this inequality also the will of God? If so, is it fair? The answer to both these questions, is 'yes'. Yet, there is scope for free will even in situations where change seems impossible. This is because you always

*Despite the fact that your
drives and dispositions are 'given'
you can choose to react either in
a positive or negative manner
That is the power of
your free will*

have your free will, and, therefore, the freedom to choose your reactions. Despite the fact that your drives and dispositions are 'given', you can choose to react in either a positive or negative manner. That is the power of your free will. How you use your free will is an important determinant of the outcomes in your life. Because, finally, you are the architect of your own destiny. Every thought, emotion, wish and action creates a force. The good and the bad both affect us and remain with us, until we balance them out.

You are the architect of your own destiny Every thought, emotion, wish and action creates a force The good and the bad both affect us and remain with us until we balance them out

Does this mean that sometimes effort can fall flat in the face of destiny? The answer given in the scriptures is, 'no'. The inner force never fails, although it may appear to be so in achieving the immediate worldly ends. It is like a person who wishes to remain physically fit by engaging in a sport. He may lose the game, but despite that, he does achieve physical fitness. In the same way, all your actions get added to the stock of your skills and strengths which can help improve your future results.

My friend Dada J P Vaswani once told me a story which I would like to share with you. During World War II, there was a Polish Air Force pilot, Roman Tursky, who while flying over Germany had to make a forced landing. He sent his plane for repairs and spent the night in a hotel. The next morning, as he stepped out of his room into the corridor of the hotel, a man came running and collided against him. The man was pale with fear as a German Secret Police team was hounding him. In a reflex action move, Roman Tursky shepherded the man into his room. Acting totally on an impulse, Roman Tursky saved the life of this unknown person.

Later, when Poland was occupied by Germany, Roman Tursky migrated to England where he joined the Royal Air Force and went on to become a war hero. In one of the sorties, Roman Tursky's plane crashed. The critically injured Roman Tursky was taken to the nearest hospital where he slipped into a coma. When after many days he regained consciousness, he found a stranger standing at his bedside, intently looking at him. The stranger asked, "Do you remember me?" "No," said Roman Tursky. The stranger said, "Years ago you saved my life and yesterday morning when I read in the newspaper about your plane crash and that you were in coma, I came here."

A creative person is motivated by his own desire to achieve not by the desire to beat others

"What for?" asked Roman Tursky. "Because," answered the stranger, "I wanted to help you. They say that I am one of the best brain surgeons in the country. I operated on you and you are fine now." So, the moral of the story is: Always do your best and leave the rest to the will of God.

A creative man is motivated by the desire to achieve, not by the desire to beat others. God wants you to focus on your own life, and use the power of your free will to improve your situation. He sends you problems and puts you in difficulties, so that you learn how to defeat and overcome them, and in the process become more evolved and a better human being.

Who is in charge

Q I enjoyed reading your book, *Turning Points,* in which you have described the important junctures in your life which steered you towards the Rashtrapati Bhawan. Apparently you made the right decisions at the important turning points in your life. What I understood from your story is that life, as it is now, is the result of our past choices and decisions.

What I want to ask is, how did you make those decisions which turned out to have such far reaching consequences? I am not very clear how such choices are actually made. How do the tendencies of our own mind influence the decisions we make when we encounter a specific event or situation? Can it be said that freedom of choice and the exercise of our free will are the most important factors in shaping a person's fate or destiny? Or, is it that tendencies already 'wired-in' into our genes stimulate certain thoughts leading us to take some specific actions under a certain set of circumstances? The question I want to put to you is, who is in charge?

The brain, the body and the genome are locked, all three, in a dance
– Matt Ridley

We live in a universe of complex network of interactions of space, time, mass, energy and consciousness. Physicist and consciousness researcher, Thomas Campbell, in his book, *My Big Theory of Everything*, proposed the idea of the universe as a 'giant brain'. According to him, the evolution of systems over time is influenced by a natural growth dynamics and this holds true for all kinds of networks, whether it is the Internet, the human brain or the universe. According to him, we as individual beings are derivative consciousnesses within a much larger pattern or interaction of being: the mind-body, family, community, environment and culture and with nobody designated as incharge. The world is full of many such intricate, intelligent and inter-connected systems that affect each other and operate without any one control centre.

Let me give you the example of an economy.

——

The world is full of intricate, intelligent and interconnected systems that affect each other and operate without any one control centre

——

Economies are very complex systems of demand and supply with diffused controls. Though there are some general rules, it is very difficult to predict the growth or decline of economies. The illusion that economies run better if somebody is put in charge of them and decides what, where, how much will be manufactured and by whom and at what price, has done devastating harm to the wealth and health of peoples all over the world.

Take another example, that of our human body. The human body is not merely a brain running a body by releasing chemicals called hormones. Neither is it a mere body running a genome by switching on hormone receptors, nor is it a genome running a brain by switching on genes that switch on hormones. Though the human body is not any one of these individual systems, yet it is all of these at once. The brain and the body are part of the same system. A hormone, called cortisol, that is made by CYP17 gene sitting over Chromosome 10, literally integrates the body and the mind by altering the configuration of the brain. Cortisol interferes with the immune system, changes the sensitivity of the ears, nose and eyes, and alters various bodily functions. The brain, responding to psychological stimuli, controls and regulates the release of cortisol. Coursing through the veins, cortisol suppresses the reactivity of the immune system facilitating a dormant viral infection to flare up or a new one to gain strength in the body. The symptoms may indeed be physical and the causes psychological. But if the brain is affected by a disease or by the consumption of alcohol or other similar substances which alter the chemistry of the brain causing moods to change, the causes are physical and the symptoms psychological.

I discussed this issue with my friend, Dr Jayesh Sheth, Founder-Chairman of the Institute of Human Genetics at Ahmedabad, who explained that switching 'on' and 'off' of human genes could be influenced by conscious or unconscious external actions. The genes that are switched on by cortisol, in turn switch on other genes, and which in turn switch on other genes and so on. But a large number of genes can remain switched 'off' through an entire life span as external events or free-willed behaviour are required to switch them 'on'. So, far from us being at the mercy of our omnipotent genes, it is often our genes that are at our mercy. It is an indisputable fact that you can trigger the 'happiness centres' of the brain with a deliberate smile as surely as you can trigger a smile with happy thoughts. If you live recklessly or are stuck in a stressful job or in a dysfunctional family, or repeatedly imagine fearful and negative things happening to you, you will raise your cortisol levels, and the cortisol will dash about within your body switching some genes 'on' and switching some others 'off'.

Man is capable of consciously fashioning his own destiny with knowledge of the good and the bad the ugly and the beautiful and the capacity to choose between them

Though God's will for humanity is indeed universal, the Holy *Quran Sharif* (76:3) ascribes a free and active role to man, 'We have shown the path to man, and he is free to choose the right path and be thankful or to choose the path of ingratitude.' It means that man is capable of consciously fashioning his own destiny with knowledge of the good and the bad, the ugly and the beautiful, and the capacity to choose between them. I can tell you from my own personal experience that God has been extremely loving and merciful to me, but I have lived a simple life of doing maximum work and minimal consumption. Although, the scope of man's will is greater and more extensive than that of all other known living creatures and plays a more creative role, man's will has effect only in those areas designated by God for his activity and deeds. Therefore, man cannot accomplish everything that he wants in his life but must flow with God's will, which envelops everything.

It often happens that a person decides to do something, but however hard he tries, he is unable to accomplish it. The reason for this is not that God's will opposes itself to the person's will and prevents him from doing what he wishes, but some unknown external factor, which lies beyond the scope of the person's knowledge and control, creates obstacles in the way and prevents him or her from attaining his goals. Conversely, sometimes we are chosen, for no apparent reason or qualification for special assignments and tasks.

Our aspirations may not be fulfilled each time But our experience of aspiring always and certainly transforms us

Both individuals and societies constantly encounter such obstacles and opportunities. Considering the fact that in the natural realm, there is no cause without an effect and no effect without a cause, and that our means of perception are limited to this world and to the human realm, it should not be difficult for us to accept that our aspirations may not be fulfilled each time. But our experience of aspiring, always and certainly, transforms us.

The process whereby larger entities, patterns, and regularities arise through interactions among smaller or simpler entities that themselves do not exhibit any such properties is called emergence. Groups of human beings, if each left free to regulate themselves tend to produce spontaneous order, rather than meaningless chaos. The stock market, or any market for that matter, is an example of emergence on a grand scale. Emergence regulates the prices of stocks and shares of companies across the world, even though there is no central planning and no one entity which controls the workings of the entire market.

If we try to live in harmony and focus our efforts to improve not only our condition but also of those around us a beautiful future would automatically emerge

So, see yourself as a part of the people around you, see yourself as a part of the larger picture and you will find your way ahead in life. Selfish pursuits, actions taken out of personal whims and fancies or because of emotional drives of anger and hatred do not take people very far. Instead, if we try to live in harmony and focus our efforts to improve not only our condition, but also of all those around us, a beautiful future would automatically emerge. All turning points in life are indeed junctures wherein God's will supersedes over human will. Sometimes we are stopped, and at times, we are the chosen one. God is in charge.

You are unique

Q Sir, you very often say that if we put our minds to it, we can achieve anything. But is that really true? Is it possible for my average child to play cricket like Sachin Tendulkar or take on the Ambani brothers in an earnings race? I am not so sure. I think that greatness, which is a combination of ability, talent and skill, is inborn in some people and that only a select few people with perfect genes and predisposed qualities can rise to greatness. This means that not everybody can be as good as Gandhiji or as brilliant as Vikram Sarabhai. Great people are born with that 'something special', which other people do not seem to have. It might be charisma or the way they look or their ability to speak powerful words; whatever it is, it seems as though it is something that cannot be developed and you either have it or you don't. I wish you had a family and we could have seen if your children inherited your genius or not. But since that is not so, I must ask this you this question.

Tell me Sir, why do some people have this natural ability and others do not? Is it something in the genes that is passed down from parent to child? Is it something to do with 'karma' and how the particular person was in his or her previous lives? Or is it something to do with the manner of their early upbringing? Or does none of this matter? I think the pursuit of greatness is completely hollow unless it is in order to help others. I am highly stressed because I do not think my life is where or what it should be. Do you ever ask yourself if you want to be different from the person you are now?

There is no greatness where there is no simplicity, goodness and truth
– Leo Tolstoy

It has long been known that certain physical characteristics such as our height, the colour of our eyes and hair, pigmentation of the skin and certain diseases are all a function of the genes we inherit; and some other physical characteristics, if not determined, at least appear to be strongly influenced by the genetic make-up of our biological parents. This has led many to speculate whether psychological characteristics such as behavioural tendencies, personality attributes and mental abilities are also 'wired-in' before our birth.

Those who adopt an extreme hereditary position are known as 'nativists'. Their basic assumption is that characteristics of the human species, as a whole, are a product of evolution and that individual differences are due to each person's unique genetic code. Characteristics and differences that are not observable at birth, but which emerge later in life, are regarded as the product of maturation. That is to say we all have an inner 'biological clock' or 'nature' which switches on or off different types of behaviour in a pre-programmed way.

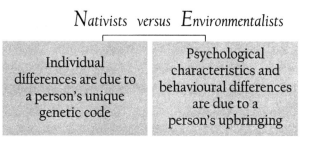

*N*ativists *versus* *E*nvironmentalists

Individual differences are due to a person's unique genetic code	Psychological characteristics and behavioural differences are due to a person's upbringing

At the other end of the spectrum are the 'environmentalists'. Their basic assumption is that at birth the human mind is a blank slate which is gradually 'filled' up as a result of the individual's experiences. From this point of view, psychological characteristics and behavioural differences that emerge through infancy and childhood are the result of learning. It is how you are brought up or 'nurtured' that governs the psychologically significant aspects of your personality development, and the concept of maturation applies only to the biological aspects of growth. So, when an infant forms an attachment he is responding to the love and attention he has received. Language is learnt from imitating the speech of others and cognitive development depends on the degree of stimulation in the environment and, more broadly, the civilization within which the child is reared.

Today, hardly anyone accepts either of the extreme positions of 'nature' versus 'nurture' or the nativists versus environmentalists. There are simply too many 'facts' on both sides of the argument, which are inconsistent with an 'all or nothing' view. That is to say, given that both genetics and environment influence the person we become, which is more important? So, instead of asking whether child development is linked to 'nature' or 'nurture', the question has been reformulated to 'how much?'

But in my view, even the question of 'how much' is a wrong question. Consider intelligence as an example. Like most types of human behaviour, intelligence is a complex, many-sided phenomenon, which manifests itself in a variety of ways. The 'how much' question assumes that the variables can all be expressed numerically and that the issue can be resolved in a quantitative manner. The reality is that 'nature' and 'nurture' interact in countless number of different and complex ways, resulting in the unique individuals that we are. If that were not so, how does one explain the different personalities that children of one set of parents grow up to be.

The reality is that 'nature' and 'nurture' interact in a countless number of different and complex ways resulting in the unique individuals that we are

This realisation is especially important given the recent advances in genetics. The Human Genome Project has stimulated enormous interest in tracing different types of behaviour to particular strands of DNA located on specific chromosomes. It is believed that scientists are on the verge of discovering (or have already discovered) the gene for criminality, for alcoholism and so on. In order to ensure that these scientific discoveries are not misused or abused, there needs to be a greater understanding of the fact that biology interacts in a very complex way with both the cultural context and the personal choices that people make about how they live their lives. There is no neat and simple way of unravelling these qualitatively different and reciprocal influences on human behaviour.

Each one of us is unique
You should enjoy and celebrate
your uniqueness
You do not have to pretend
to be what you are not
Treasure your uniqueness
It is a gift given only to you

To your question, whether I ever wish to be different from what I am now, my answer is no, I do not. I am what I am because of the circumstances of my life and the efforts that I have put in. Each one of us is unique. You should enjoy and celebrate your uniqueness. You do not have to pretend to be what you are not or to seem more like someone else, because you weren't meant to be like someone else. You do not have to conceal the parts of you that are not like what you see in someone else, because you were meant to be different.

You were meant to be you. Nowhere in the entire world will the same thoughts be going through in anyone's mind, soul and spirit as are going through in yours right now, and neither will there be the same set of circumstances or the same identical set of events

The gift of yourself
was given to you
to enjoy and share
Give yourself away
Maximize your life

as in your life. If you did not exist, there would be a hole in creation, a gap in history, something missing from the plan for humankind. Treasure your uniqueness. It is a gift given only to you.

No one can reach out to others in the unique way that you do. No one can comfort the way you do. No one can convey your warmth. No one can bring your kind of understanding to another person. No one can be cheerful and lighthearted and joyous the way you are. No one can smile your smile. No one else can bring the whole unique impact of you to another human being. Share your uniqueness. Let it be free to flow out amongst your family and friends and people you meet in the rush and clutter of everyday living. The gift of yourself was given to you to enjoy and share. Give yourself away! Maximize your life.

Wings of fire

Q India is a youthful nation. One of the most important stories of contemporary India is the rise of its young people as knowledge workers and how this has helped script its global recognition as an information technology power.

Though India's economic liberalisation, which started in 1991, has created many opportunities for high-skilled workers, there has not been a corresponding boom in manufacturing to create low-skilled jobs. There are hardly any employment opportunities for unskilled workers who do not have much education. Such young people often have no choice but to stay in low-paying jobs as rickshaw pullers, street vendors or domestic help. Many of them do not even have these options. They just draw on whatever little their parents have and spend their time loafing around, just indulging in 'time-pass'. Young people with no opportunities or resources naturally find it difficult to get ahead in life, get married and have a family. What is your solution to this serious sociological problem?

To accomplish great things, we must not only act, but also dream; not only plan, but also believe
– Anatole France

The solution to the sociological problem of idle thoughts and destructive actions is education. Education gives youth the wings to fly. It is important that youth invest their prime years in getting good education and learning useful skills. Once the energies of the mind are channelled into productive skills and positive thoughts, there is bound to be achievement. But education by itself is not enough to overcome the obstacles and hardships of life, you have to be very determined and committed to achieving your goals and be willing to endure hardships along the way.

Youth is the embodiment of energy. It is not possible for civilization to move forward without the fresh energy, new thoughts and the courage of youth. Conversely stated, it is not possible for civilization to move backwards while there is youth in the world. The Scottish dramatist and novelist, James M. Barrie (1860 - 1937) has so beautifully

The solution to the sociological problem of idle thoughts and destructive actions is education Education gives youth the wings to fly

said, 'Youth is the joy, the little bird that has broken out of the egg and is eagerly waiting to spread out its wings in the open sky of freedom and hope'. How true! Dreams of young boys and girls float on an impatient wind, a wind that wants to create a new order; an order of strength with the energy of fire.

I, too, was once young and headstrong. My first dream was to get out of the isolation of Rameswaram island and its poor living conditions. My father understood my yearnings and encouraged me to move out and pursue my studies. There was no school beyond the primary level in Rameswaram, so at the age of twelve, I left home to study at Schwartz High School in Ramanatha- puram. As I had very little money I had to learn how to survive on a tight budget.

All during my student days what kept me going was my dream to achieve something big my desire to live a better life and my commitment to a disciplined way of living

I opted for vegetarian meals at the school canteen instead of the non-vegetarian meals which I had been used to at home, since that meant a saving of three rupees every week. Three rupees a week seems a very paltry amount now, but in those days it was a princely sum! I was ready for all kinds of hardships if it meant saving money and putting less burden on my family. Eating vegetarian food, I gradually started enjoying it, and till today I continue to be a vegetarian.

Though I came from a small place, I never felt small in any way and always had big dreams. After finishing my high school, I moved to Tiruchirapalli where I got admission in St. Joseph's College. I lived in a single pair of clothing and shoes, wearing them for as long as was possible. Only when the first pair of clothing and shoes would be completely worn out, would I get a new set. In 1954, when I decided to enroll for Aeronautical Engineering at the Madras Institute of Technology, my sister had to sell two of her gold bangles to pay for my admission fee. Here too, I lived on scholarship for my sustenance. All during my student days, what kept me going was my dream to achieve something big, my desire to live a better life, and my commitment to a disciplined way of living. Discipline is indeed the bridge between goals and accomplishments in life.

Discipline is the bridge between goals & accomplishments

Based on my own experience of life, I can tell you that there are four proven steps which will help you achieve success: one, by the age of twenty years you must define your aim in life; two, have a passion for continuously acquiring knowledge through great books, great teachers and great human beings; three, follow a disciplined lifestyle of hard work towards fulfilment of your aim; and four, persevere and persist on your chosen path.

I am greatly inspired by the life of Martin Luther King Jr., leader of the African-American Civil Rights Movement. In his famous speech, 'I have a dream', he shared his dream and his vision with the entire world. And he worked, struggled and made great personal sacrifices to see his dream come true. If he had not envisioned that dream, he would not have accomplished in his life all that which he did.

The youth hopes for a world free of poverty, unemployment, inequality and exploitation. They hope for a world free of discrimination on the grounds of race, colour, language and gender. For the youth, the world has always been full of creative challenges and opportunities. It is important that we don't allow pessimism and cynicism to dampen this hope. The positive hopes and dreams of the youth must be converted into reality. The onus of this rests in a great measure on the government, by way of providing education, job opportunities and avenues for personal growth and development.

But there are some roles and responsibilities which the youth must commit to. Specifically, there are three roles that the Indian youth has to play, but which, I feel they are failing to play. First, is the role that the youth can play in politics. Youth participation in politics is important because youth represents the country's future and its power. Youth has the ability to recognise problems and suggest solutions for them. It is a very strong force in social movements. On my Facebook page, 90 per cent of the participants are young people, mostly high school and college

The attitude of 'let things be' or what is popularly known as 'chalta hai' is a major impediment to our country's development

going students. They can educate the people around them, help them attain a higher level of intellectual ability and become productive adults.

Second, I think the Indian youth can play an important role in solving the country's unemployment problem. They should aspire to be entrepreneurs and provide jobs to other young people, rather than become workers or job seekers themselves.

Third, is the role the youth can play in bringing about change. Generally, young people have an indifferent attitude towards things, situations and politics. The attitude of 'let things be' or what is popularly known as the *chalta hai* attitude is proving fatal to India's development. This lack of spirit to press for, and bring about, change is a major impediment to our country's development. Youth embodies the prime of human strength and the peak of aspiration. Youth should not accept any compromise or lower their sights. A society that makes its youth crawl in conformity and enforces dogmas on their aspirations can never flourish.

Youth should not accept any compromise or lower their sights A society that makes its youth crawl in conformity and enforces dogmas on their aspirations can never flourish

India can become a developed nation only if everyone, especially the youth, contributes to the best of his or her capacity and ability.

There is nothing like 'time-pass' in nature One has to grow or decay move on or perish swim or drown

There is nothing like 'time-pass' in nature. One has to grow or decay, move on or perish, swim or drown. India can become a truly great nation only with the full utilisation of its youth.

Each one of us has 'wings of fire'. Education, skills and attitude provide these spiritual wings which will indeed take you to achieving great heights in your career and life.

Jalal-ud-Din Muhammad Rumi, (1207-1273) more popularly known as Rumi, was a 13th century Persion poet and Sufi mystic. The youth can adopt as their inspiration these lines written by him:

I am born with potential
I am born with goodness and trust
I am born with ideas and dreams
I am born with greatness
I am born with confidence
I am born with courage
I will defeat the problem and succeed
I am born with wings
So, I am not meant for crawling
I have wings, I will fly
I will fly and fly

Creating
a better society

The growing
influence of social media

Q Sir, I have been following your Facebook page
www.facebook.com/kalambillionbeats right
from its inception. You have been amongst the
first leaders in our country to engage young people
through social media. In the newly emerging
environment of social media, a transformation has
recently taken place in the political system. What
is your view about the influence of social media
on our electoral system? Will social media be a
game changer for Indian politics?

*We are continuously challenged by new works of culture
and, in the process, humanity evolves
– APJ Abdul Kalam*

Social media has emerged as a vital tool of communication and
has created new ways of mobilising public opinion and

encouraging participation in political and civic activities, especially among young people. There is a general euphoria over social networking as a political tool. An increasing tele-density, especially in urban areas, has spurred a huge jump in the number of people who are active online. As the middle class expands, more Indians are expected to get online. The 80 million Facebook users in India are not oblivious to politics. The general feeling is that politics needs to adapt to the new habits and lifestyle of this emerging and rapidly growing segment of population which is very active on the social media.

This is the age of the Internet. The numbers affirm the fact that Internet in India is becoming inclusive, which augurs well for the society at large. In 2013, the Internet user base grew to 213 million, up by 42 per cent, from 150 million in 2012. Of the total user base, mobile Internet users accounted for 130 million. Before the 2014 General Elections it was predicted that out of India's 543 parliamentary constituencies, results in 160 constituencies would be significantly influenced by the number of Facebook users in those constituencies. The results of the elections confirmed this. I believe that social media affected the results in 30 to 40 per cent of the overall seats. This number could go up to 60 per cent by the 2019 General Elections. In many constituencies, social media was amongst the top three communication tools, overtaking traditional methods of promotion and advertising.

In their book, *Connected: The Surprising Power of Our Social Networks and How They Shape Our Lives*, authors Nicholas Christakis and James Fowler highlight four key rules of the modern interconnected world. The first is, The Rule of Transitivity, according to which the number of connections that we have affects the quality of our life. It influences our expectations, our aspirations, our emotions and our health. The second is, The Rule of Imitation, which states that we copy our friends. Friends give us 'permission' and safety to do things. If a friend has done something, bought something, been somewhere, then we are much more likely to also do that, buy what he or she has bought and go where our friends have been. The third is, The Rule of

Rules of the interconnected world

1
Rule of Transitivity
The number of connections we have affects the quality of our life

2
Rule of Imitation
We copy our friends

3
Rule of Echo
We are affected by friends of our friends, and also by their friends

4
Rule of Transience
Networks have a life of their own

Echo, which states that we are not only affected by our friends, but also by their friends, as well as the friends of their friends. Thus, what we do echoes through three levels of friends before it loses its energy and impact. The fourth is, The Rule of Transience, which states that networks have a life of their own. No one controls or owns the network. It is complex, dynamic

Social media has sparked a realisation amongst the people that they have a voice People are able like never before to exert the pressure of their opinion on the government

and constantly evolving. There is no central control point but rather a 'shared intelligence'. For example, Wikipedia is an open system that anyone can edit. What is interesting is that it has no centralised control and like many self-organising teams with no formal authority, manages to resist abuse by applying self-policing and peer-group pressure.

Social media has proved to be a game changer for Indian politics and will be an even stronger influence in the future. Politicians are learning the potential of the online medium which, acts as an 'accelerator' in conveying their messages to the public. It already plays a big role in election campaigns in countries such as the United States and is beginning to do so in India as well. But it is a double-edged sword, because if you convey a wrong message, then in no time you are discarded by the online audience.

For the first time in the history of the world, the future of any nation is within the grasp of its people. People are able, like

Through the democratisation of content and ideas we can once again unite around common passions inspire movements and ignite change

never before, to exert pressure of their opinions on the leaders, be it the officials in the government or representatives in the legislature. Social media has indeed sparked a realisation amongst the people that they have a

Politicians are learning the potential of the online medium which acts as an 'accelerator' in conveying their messages to the public

voice, and through the democratisation of content and ideas, they can once again unite around common passions, inspire movements and ignite change.

Inculcating righteousness

Q Sir, I heard you talking about how children can use their love to prevent their parents from indulging in corruption. But the reality is that there is so much corruption in every aspect of our life and it is almost impossible to avoid it. Most of us do not want to indulge in any corrupt practices, but the system has become such that even an honest person is forced to become corrupt. I know that my father is honest and does not believe in doing anything wrong or going against the law. But I feel that he does certain things which he may not personally believe in or agree with, but as part of a larger system, he has to do them in order to survive.

In this scenario, I shudder to think what would be my future. Given the circumstances which my father is facing, I am not sure what sort of person I would turn out to be when I grow up and how

I would face a similar situation. Please tell me, Sir, what can I do to ensure that I don't end up in the situation that my father is in?

No other feeling in the soul of person can bring the joy and happiness than that of knowing you are doing all you can to become righteous
–William R Bradford

These days many people do not ascribe any morality to their actions, they believe that their actions have only social or economic consequences. The general thinking is that there is nothing which is either right or wrong and the action which is best suited to the situation must be taken. Each one of us, at one time or the other, has heard the statement, "Okay, have it your own way," and so is the way that many in the world live. Therefore, I am not surprised at your question. But let me tell you, there is a better way. That is, to live a life of righteousness.

There is great simplicity in righteousness. In every situation that we confront in life, there is either a right way or a wrong way to proceed. If we choose the right way, we are sustained in our actions by the principles of righteousness, in which there is power from the heavens above. If we choose the wrong way and act on that choice, there is no

> *There is great simplicity in righteousness In every situation that we confront there is either a right way or a wrong way to proceed*

such heavenly power, we are alone and destined to fail.

The question arises: How do we know which is right and which is wrong? The system of prayer is organised as a communication system to transmit concepts of truth into the minds of human beings. God, through our conscience, *ruh* or spirit enlightens our minds and gives us clarity of understanding of the concepts of truth. This is the way God teaches us right from wrong. If we are willing to learn His ways and follow them, we will never have to guess and will always know for sure the difference between right and wrong.

Each one of us lives with his or her unique situation. There are challenges with health, money, literacy, singleness, loneliness, oppression, abuse, transgression, and a never-ending list of existing conditions. The solution to all these challenges is righteousness. In righteousness, there is the fulfilment of faith and hope. Every blessing that God has promised to His children is predicated upon obedience to His laws and commandments. Obedience to His laws and commandments is what makes us righteous, and that righteousness qualifies us to be worthy of the promised blessings.

In His benevolence, God has given us the law of repentance. Whenever there is disobedience to God's laws and commandments, the option of repentance is open to us. If we act upon this marvellous law, we will be forgiven for our disobedience and we can decide to become more righteous; thus repentance leads us to righteousness. In fact, most of the challenges that we have in morality can be solved by repentance and finally by righteousness. All religions in the world teach this very basic truth.

There is great joy and happiness in striving to live righteously. In simple terms, the plan of God for His children is that they come to this earth and do all that they can to learn and live in obedience to His laws. With this, comes inner peace and comfort that, in doing all we can, the plan of God is being accomplished. No other feeling can bring joy and happiness to your soul than that of knowing you are doing all you can to live righteously.

There is no right way to do a wrong thing Righteousness is not only the better of many ways righteousness is the only way

In a world where transgression, corruption, and terrorism strike fear into men and women, where can we turn to for safety and security? There is no safety and security except in righteousness. There is no place to hide. There are no walls to keep out the adversary and his campaign of opposition. Other than righteousness, there is no defence against the uncertain and unknown. Fear in the hearts and minds of men and women can be turned to peace only by replacing it with an understanding of God's plan of happiness and the knowledge that they are doing all they can to become righteous and worthy to qualify for eternal salvation. With it, we bind with God.

There is no right way to do a wrong thing. Righteousness is not only the better of many other ways, righteousness is the only way. Righteousness has the power to provide the joy and happiness, the safety and security that people long for, and have searched for throughout the generations of mankind. It seems like such a simple solution, but the reality is that the Satan is abroad in the land, and he goes forth deceiving people and nations. There is opposition to the righteous path. But the reality is that right and wrong do exist. Our actions do have moral consequences.

Bruce Lipton, in his groundbreaking book in the field of new biology, *The Biology of Belief*, explains that the evolution of higher mammals into humans brought forth a new level of awareness called 'self-consciousness'. The subconscious mind is our 'autopilot', and the conscious mind is our manual control. The subconscious mind is one of the most powerful information processors ever known. It observes both the surrounding world and the body's internal awareness, reads the environmental cues and immediately engages with the righteous course of action - all without the help, supervision or even awareness of the conscious mind. The need is to strengthen the subconscious mind and try to be tuned into it and to follow it. This can be done through prayer. As Florence Nightingale, the pioneer of modern nursing wrote, 'Often when people seem unconscious, a word of prayer reaches them'. Prayer has the power of connecting us more deeply to our subconscious mind and when we follow the path indicated by the subconscious mind, we are on the path of righteousness.

Republic of cash

Q Sir, is corruption not India's biggest problem today? Leaders like Mahatma Gandhi sacrificed their lives for the country's independence but today many people are misusing their powers. There is corruption at all levels and in every sphere of life, with common people having to face corruption in their day-to-day life. Bureaucracy and the problem of corruption seem to be entwined, with government officials at all levels asking for favours, and often receiving them from companies that do not want to suffer delays in receiving licences or other official approvals. For example, when a minor bureaucrat asks an applicant to arrange for a car to visit his family in another state, it is accepted as the price of doing business, but a similar request in the USA would be met with shocked and outright rejection. Eight anti-corruption bills have been pending before the Indian Parliament but it seems to be

fractured in its attempts to get them passed. Is moral decadence the price an entrepreneur must pay?

Corruption has its own motivations, and one has to thoroughly study that phenomenon and eliminate the foundations that allow corruption to exist. Corruption emanates from the feeling of 'what you can give me'. This thought has to replaced by 'what can I give' through proper education and family tradition
– APJ Abdul Kalam

I fully agree with you that our country, where leaders such as Mahatma Gandhi, Sardar Patel, Lal Bahadur Shastri and Kamraj were born and led a value-based life, is now facing the problem of widespread corruption. Nowadays corruption can be seen everywhere. It is like a cancer afflicting our public life. When we talk of corruption in public life, it covers corruption in politics, state governments, central government, business and industry. Corruption is most evident in government offices which involve public dealings. If somebody does not pay for the work, then he or she can be sure that the work will get delayed or may not be done.

People have developed an insatiable appetite for money and they can go to any length for it. Undoubtedly, they talk of morality and the importance of a value-based life, but that is just for public consumption. Their inner voice is something else. It is always crying for money. Often it has been seen that the very officers who are deputed to look into matters of corruption turn out to be corrupt themselves. Our leaders, too, are no less. Thus the network of corruption continues unchecked.

The causes of corruption in India include excessive regulations, complicated taxes and licencing systems, multiplicity of government departments with opaque bureaucracy and discretionary powers, monopoly by government controlled institutions on certain goods and delivery of services, and the lack of transparent laws and processes.

Everybody knows that criminals have no morals, hence nothing good can be expected from them. But the police, who are supposed to be the symbol of law and order and discipline, even some of them indulge in corruption. This is more so because they enjoy unlimited powers, and often no action is taken against them even

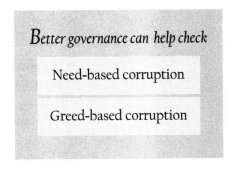

though there are complaints and sufficient proof of abuse of office, atrocities and high-handedness.

An income and wealth distribution based on corruption does not encourage the kind of effort that builds real wealth. Instead, effort goes into bribing and otherwise influencing corrupt decision makers. Not only do effort and personal investment decisions get distorted, it leads to sub-optimal results at the national level. Suppose, in a bid, corruption leads to inefficient allocations of rights (to land, minerals, spectrum or other resources). The ones who get the rights, get them because either they are the most corrupt or most able to bribe, and not because they will be the most efficient users of these resources. Resources are thus misused and output is lower than what it could and should be, leading to a national loss.

Corruption can be need-based or greed-based. Better governance can at least help to check need-based corruption as clear policies and procedures will make the process of seeking clearances, approvals and renewals, transparent and streamlined. Better governance can also check greed-based corruption because punishment for the corrupt would be effective and prompt in a better-governed country. Immediate and effective steps should be taken to correct the overall situation. Declarations of property and assets of government employees should be made compulsory and routine checks along with surprise inspections and raids should be conducted at regular intervals.

Reducing corruption will not only guarantee growth but it seems to be a necessary condition for sustained growth

Though it seems very difficult to control corruption, it is not impossible. It is not only the responsibility of the government, but of citizens too. Other countries have made transitions from endemic corruption to societies where honesty and hard work pay off. Reducing corruption will not only guarantee growth, but it seems to be a necessary condition for sustaining that growth.

There will have to be joint effort if we want to eliminate corruption. We must follow some principles so that we may be models for the coming generations. Let us take a pledge to create an atmosphere free from corruption. That will be our biggest achievement as citizens of our country.

Youth have the power to stop corruption. The youth can bring about a change by advocating clean habits. In every household, if children can stop their parents from bribing others or accepting bribes, then the society would soon be corruption-free. It is in the family where corruption starts. It is in the family wherein the movement to cleanse our society will need to start. A cleansed family environment and the recently approved Lokpal Bill will help in eliminating corruption from our country.

The importance
of the joint family

Q Sir, I read your book, *Family and Nation,* written along with Acharya Mahapragya which promotes the idea of the joint family system. My observation, Sir, is that with changing gender roles, greater inter-country mobility because of better employment opportunities and technological advances, the concept of a joint family is on the decline. Interdependence on each other in large families seems to be getting replaced by independent living and a self-sufficient attitude.

Living together under one roof, which was all about shared values and harmonious co-existence, today raises issues of 'adjustment' and 'compromise'. After marriage, many couples prefer to live away from their in-laws and relatives to avoid what they call an 'intrusion' into their conjugal space, whereas a few decades ago this concept did not even exist!

I am an endocrinologist and I attribute my successful medical career to my joint family. During my professional training period, it was the voluntary decision of my family and my parents-in-law to stay with me and look after my child that allowed me to carve out a fulfilling career.

As a doctor, I have observed that patients who come from a joint family recover better than others. A greater percentage of couples who come to psychologists and doctors to discuss their disintegrating marriage is from nuclear families as they don't have family members and elders to turn to for support.

Sir, only you can tell the older generation to respect the autonomy of a couple and not impose diktats that may impede their relationship. Dictatorship and mentorship are two separate things and should never be confused. Medical research shows that more than diets, exercise, genes or location, it is a family-oriented lifestyle that ensures a healthy life. Please start a social movement.

Family means no one gets left behind or forgotten
–David Ogden Stiers

Throughout recorded history, in every culture, the family has been the fundamental building block of society but today, judging by many yardsticks, the family seems to be in crisis.

In industrialised societies, changing economic conditions and new patterns of consumption have led to an increase in the number of families where both parents work, leaving less time for children and family life. High divorce rates have created a culture of marital insecurity. Other social forces have served to decrease support from the extended family, the workplace, neighbours and society at large. In the developing world, such trends are compounded by the over-arching problems of poverty, environmental degradation, inequalities between women and men, and the rise of global pandemics, in particular HIV/AIDS.

In our book, Acharya Mahapragyaji and I have projected the family as the foundation of a nation. We have presented the human person as the agent and beneficiary of development and emphasised the importance of empowerment, participation and inclusiveness. The family is the basic unit of society and its strength is integral and central to all development.

Strong families are indeed central to the overall effort to improve social and economic development, create sustainable communities and increase global prosperity. For the individual, of course, a strong family provides many benefits. The family is the most basic support system for its members and is a fortification against hard times. People in strong families are healthier, happier and better adjusted.

In terms of social development in general, and the overall advancement of civilization, the family is of primary importance. For it is in the family that basic values of morality are formed. It is in the family that the essential capacities for learning, self-confidence and positive social interactions are acquired. And it is from the base of a strong family that individuals are best able to contribute to society.

Religion has historically been one of the most important factors in family cohesion. Laws of marriage, divorce, the rearing of children, the values to be transmitted have all traditionally come from religion. Today, however, the connection between religion and the family is under assault. First and foremost, the male-dominated, authoritarian model for the family structure has become widely discredited, and rightly so. Associated with the oppression of women, inflexible child-rearing practices, and the preservation of masculine power, this model of family life is now seen as unhealthy and unjust.

The importance of family

It is in the family that basic values of morality are formed

It is in the family that capacities for learning, self-confidence and positive social interactions are acquired

It is from the base of a strong family that individuals are best able to contribute to society

The failure of the male-dominated, authoritarian model has given rise to an alternative in many Western countries. More liberal and secular in its orientation, it, rightly gives women a more equal role in family decisions. At the same time, however, this model has largely discarded the firm sense of morality offered by religious teachings, opening the door to a kind of permissiveness in child-rearing, that all too often leaves children with no firm sense of values or ethical construct other than self-gratification.

It is hard to imagine building a successful world civilization on such values. So what is the alternative? You have asked me to start a social movement. I don't really know if I can do that, but I definitely advocate equality and mutuality in the relationship between husband and wife, while at the same time, outlining a well-defined understanding of the rights and responsibilities between parents and children. In such a family, the power and indulgence-based practices of control, competition, and excessive individualism and independence give way to those of equality, cooperation, universality and interdependence.

> *Family is the basic unit of society and its strength is integral and central to all development in the economy*

Also, one has to realise that the definition of joint family is changing continuously. The joint family members now include friends and neighbours who are connected with mobile telephones and other electronic devices. A joint family system has the inherent capacity to solve problems when they occur whereas in the nuclear families the problems become very severe since this problem-solving mechanism is missing. Therefore, in my opinion the joint family system, particularly for India, is very suitable.

The queen of virtues

Q Sir, I was very touched when I heard you saying that every year your go to visit your teacher, Reverend Father Chinnadurai, who taught you physics at St. Joseph's College, Tiruchirappalli, between 1950 and 1954. It moved me to tears and I have no words to describe this profound sense of gratitude that, you as a student, have for your teacher.

Unfortunately, there is an utter lack of gratitude these days. Two places where gratitude seems to be missing the most are, home and work. My husband assumes that I know he appreciates what I am doing, and so he does not bother to ever appreciate or thank me. Likewise, my two kids think it is my sovereign duty to be at their beck and call, night and day, so why should I get any thanks for doing my duty? It is a similar story at the workplace. My manager rarely says a thank you, even though I may have put exceptional effort into my work.

Hurt and resentment have built up in me because of this obvious lack of recognition and appreciation. But, when you explained that gratitude goes much further than thankfulness, I understood how we can each, teach one another the value of gratitude by bringing out the best within us, and thereby the finest in others.

My question to you is, what should be done if our efforts fail to create any grateful response in others?

Gratitude takes us outside of ourselves where we see ourselves as part of a larger, intricate network of sustaining relationships
— Robert Emmons

I agree with you that these days gratitude has become detached from its moral bearings and collectively, we are worse off because of this. When the Roman philosopher Cicero (106 BC-43 BC) stated that gratitude was the queen of virtues, he most assuredly did not mean that gratitude was merely a stepping-stone towards personal happiness. Gratitude is a morally complex disposition, and reducing this virtue to a technique or strategy to improve one's mood or to get a 'feel-good' feeling is doing it an injustice. Similarly, restricting gratitude to just an inner feeling is insufficient.

In the history of ideas, gratitude is considered to be an action. For example, returning a favour is not only virtuous in itself, but is valuable to society. To reciprocate is the right thing to do. 'There is no duty more indispensable than that of returning a kindness,' said Cicero. Seneca said, 'He who receives a benefit with gratitude

We lack a sense of gratitude for the freedoms that we enjoy and we lack gratitude towards those who lost their lives in the fight for freedom

repays the first instalment on his debt.' Across time, ingratitude has been treated as a serious vice. In fact, ingratitude is a greater vice than gratitude is a virtue. Ingratitude is the 'essence of vileness', wrote the great German philosopher Immanuel Kant (1724-1804). Scottish philosopher David Hume (1711-1776) opined that ingratitude is 'the most horrible and unnatural crime that a person is capable of committing'.

Gratitude does matter for, and contributes to, happiness. Bruce Lipton, in his book, *Biology of Belief*, established the link between gratitude and happiness. Based on evidence he documented from childhood to old age, the wide array of psychological, physical and relational benefits associated with gratitude. Gratitude is important not only because it helps people feel good, but also because it inspires them to do good. Gratitude heals, energises and transforms lives in many ways, consistent with the notion that virtue is its own reward, and also produces other rewards.

In my experience, dispositional gratitude is positively associated with qualities such as empathy, forgiveness and the willingness to help others. For example, people who have a grateful disposition show their empathetic behaviour at the work place and provide emotional support to their colleagues. When people report feeling grateful, thankful and appreciative they also feel more loving, forgiving, joyful and enthusiastic. Notably, family members, friends, partners and colleagues consistently report that people who practise gratitude are viewed as more helpful, outgoing, optimistic and trustworthy.

A spirit of ingratitude corrodes human relationships and becomes endemic within a culture when entitlements and rights are prioritised over duties and obligations

On a macro level, gratitude is the adhesive that binds members of a society together. One just needs to try and imagine human relationships existing without gratitude. Gratitude is a foundational component of the moral capital needed for a society to flourish. In my view, the virtue of gratitude is not only a firewall of protection against corruption of relationships, it also contributes positively to friendship and civility. Gratitude mitigates toxic emotions and curbs anti-social impulses and destructive interpersonal behaviour.

Gratitude requires effort. It does not always come easily or naturally and therefore grateful behaviour and thoughts often remain theoretical concepts. To convert them into action requires wilful and deliberate action. A growing number of social commentators contend that gratitude is a diminishing virtue in modern times and that we are less grateful now than in other historical periods. A spirit of ingratitude corrodes human relationships and becomes endemic within a culture when entitlements and rights are prioritised over duties and obligations. Is it any wonder then, that the biggest fear which parents now have for their children is, the frustration and resentment that may set in when life fails to deliver what the children think they are entitled to.

Gratitude is consistent with the notion that virtue is its own reward and also produces other rewards

More accurately, gratitude is about remembering and so I go to visit Reverend Father Ladislaus Chinnadurai whenever it is possible. If there is a crisis of gratitude in contemporary life, it is because we are collectively forgetful. We have lost a sense of gratitude about the freedoms we enjoy, a lack of gratitude towards those who lost their lives in the fight for freedom, and a lack of gratitude for all the material advantages we have. On the other hand, grateful people draw upon positive memories of being the recipients of benevolence, a giftedness that is neither earned nor deserved. More than the memory of the mind, gratitude is the memory of the heart, it is the way that the heart remembers. The memory of the heart includes the memory of those we are dependent on, just as the forgetfulness of dependence is the unwillingness or inability to remember the benefits provided by others.

Gratitude is important not only because it helps people feel good but also because it inspires them to do good

We have come to this planet as unique creatures bestowed with the power to imagine. It is 'expected' of every human being to 'understand' the unity of all that exists in this universe. Every

> *Gratitude is the*
> *memory of the heart*
> *It is the way that*
> *the heart remembers*

thing is interconnected and supports one another. A life cannot be meaningful without this realisation. We are all walking on an evolutionary path, becoming a better person each day. So keep giving whatever you can, for this is the only way forward. Give your time to good deeds, help others who are in a less fortunate condition, and if nothing else, give respect to their presence around you. Never shun them. You will soon realise that when your efforts fail to create any grateful response in others, it is their failure and you are merely being used as a means to put them to test.

Giving is good

Q Sir, I read your speech titled, 'What can I give?' Your speech was full of idealism and very inspiring and it would be wonderful if we all behaved in the manner that you described in your speech. But sadly, the reality on the ground is very different. I want to share with you the impracticalities of following your advice. For today's young generation, there is less of black and white, and more of grey. The inclination is towards pragmatism and not idealism. The emphasis is on taking and not giving. All around us we see people, all the time, 'taking' what they can from society, from the 'system'. Whether it be the contractor who makes the road, or the person who wins a big tender for a national-level project, the emphasis is always or how they can 'give less' into the system, whether by putting in less or inferior quality of material, and how they can 'take' more out, by saving costs and thereby increasing their profits. Tell me Sir, when the tendency is to take whatever is there to be 'taken', how can I be 'giving' all the time?

Though giving is a difficult challenge, it is the only way to evolve. Give so that you can grow
– APJ Abdul Kalam

My elder brother, APJ Muhammad Muthu Meera Lebbai Maracayer, is 98 years old and lives in our ancestral home in Rameswaram. Every Friday, he takes a small bundle of currency notes, about one thousand rupees, and distributes them to the poor people around the mosque. People make it a point to receive from him not because it would make a great material difference in their lives, but because they feel a sense of something special, something deeper than just the physical act of giving and taking.

Interactions between psychological processes and the nervous and immune systems of the human body are studied in Psycho-Neuro-Immunology (PNI). My friend, William Selvamurthy, briefed me about the emerging research in this field. There are credible studies that attest to the benefits of giving, not just for the recipients but also for the givers' health and happiness, and for strengthening of entire communities. Selvamurthy says givers always benefit from giving, whether it is donating to charities, giving blankets in winter to a homeless shelter, or distributing water to passer-bys and animals during summer or volunteering their time. I, too, believe in giving, and there are five valid reasons for giving and the benefits that flow from it.

First and foremost, giving makes us feel happy. These good feelings are reflected in our biology. When people give to charities, it activates regions of the brain associated with pleasure, social connection and trust, creating a 'warm glow' effect. Scientists believe that altruistic behaviour releases endorphins in the brain, which produce positive feelings. On 18 December 2005, I visited Mata Amritanandamayi Math in Kollam district in Kerela, where along with Amma, I participated in a function for giving away five hundred newly constructed houses for the tsunami-affected citizens. The 'warm glow' effect on Amma's face was so very evident.

Giving promotes cooperation and social connections. When you give you are more likely to get back

Secondly, giving is good for our health. A wide range of research has linked different forms of generosity to better health, even among the sick and elderly. In his book, *Why Good Things Happen to Good People*, Stephen Post reports that giving to others has been shown to increase health benefits in people with chronic illness. Elderly people who did volunteer work were found to live longer and healthier lives than those who did not engage in volunteering. One reason that giving may improve physical health and longevity is that it helps decrease stress which is associated with a variety of health problems. There is a direct physiological benefit to those who give. My brother is a good example.

Thirdly, giving promotes cooperation and social connections. When you give, you are more likely to get back. When you give to others, your generosity is likely to be rewarded by others down the line, sometimes by the person you give to, sometimes by someone else. These exchanges promote a sense of trust and cooperation that strengthen our ties to others, and research shows that having positive social interactions is central to good mental and physical health. What is more, when we give to others, we do not only make them feel close to us, we also feel close to them. Being kind and generous leads you to perceive others more positively and more charitably, and this fosters a heightened sense of interdependence and cooperation in the social community.

> *Giving evokes gratitude*
> *Cultivating gratitude in*
> *everyday life is one of*
> *the keys to increasing*
> *personal happiness*

Fourth, giving evokes gratitude. Whether you are on the giving or the receiving end of a gift, that gift can elicit feelings of gratitude. It can be a way of expressing gratitude or instilling gratitude in the recipient. I personally experienced how gratitude is integral to happiness, health, and social bonding. In the 1990s, Dr Hardwar Singh, my colleague at the Defence Research and Development Organisation, needed a life-saving liver transplant. I fought through the system to ensure that he was sent to UK to receive the transplant. Today, he is living a healthy and happy life. When you express your gratitude in words or actions, you not only boost your own positivity but also of other people's. Cultivating gratitude in everyday life is one of the keys to increasing personal happiness.

Finally, giving is contagious. When we give, we not only help the immediate recipient of our gift, rather, it triggers a ripple effect of generosity throughout the community. When one person behaves generously, it inspires others to also behave generously. In fact, giving can spread by three degrees, from the first person to the second person, and from the second to the third. As a result, each person in a network can influence dozens or even hundreds of people, some of whom he or she may not even know. In 2003, I gave a small sum to the Care Foundation to start a fund for poor children suffering from congenital heart disease to receive life-saving heart surgeries. The fund has now grown to 3 crore rupees and more than a thousand children have benefited from it.

Giving is contagious When we give we not only help the recipient of our gift it also triggers a ripple effect of generosity throughout the community

So whether you buy gifts, volunteer your time, or donate money to charity, your giving is much more than a just momentary emotion of feel-good. It can help you build stronger social connections and even jumpstart a cascade of generosity through your community. And do not be surprised if you find yourself benefiting from a big dose of happiness in the process. By speaking the truth, by not becoming angry and by giving when asked, even if it be a little, you can indeed transform your life and benefit those living around you.

World without art
is like a balloon without air

Q The middle school in our town has no art classes. I find this very upsetting because I know that art can be a great source of comfort and achievement especially for children who are wired a little differently. I have a son who is a bit slow in learning, and as he struggles with controlling his expressions in his classes, the teachers often get impatient and irritated. He ends up getting into trouble for his chatty comments, silly answers or just plain lack of attention. I read in a book about your work with Father George at Anna University and learnt that pursuing creative arts is a form of expression that comforts and relaxes the mind and helps rejuvenate under-developed cells in the brain.

Sir, there are many forms of art such as painting, music, theatre, woodwork, sculpture, photography that can help children like my son. It is very sad and disgraceful that our schools do not offer any of these options. Can we not use arts in our schools to develop the latent strengths of a child and use them as a bridge for understanding the abstractions of his mind?

A broad education in the arts, helps give children a better understanding of their world. We need students who are culturally literate as well as math and science literate
–APJ Abdul Kalam

Evidence of the usefulness of arts in compensating for lost competencies in mentally challenged children was clearly borne out in the studies that Father George and I did. It also showed that engagement in fine arts is beneficial in the educational process. The arts help in development of neural networks in the brain that produce a broad spectrum of benefits ranging from fine motor skills to creativity and improved emotional balance. One must realise that these systems often take months and even years to fine-tune. The arts enhance the process of learning. The systems they nourish, which include our integrated sensory, attention, cognitive, emotional and motor capacities are, in fact, the driving forces behind all other learning.

Your question that why arts in our schools cannot be used to develop latent personal strengths in meaningful ways and to act as a bridge for understanding the difficult abstractions of a child's mind, made me think about the very purpose of education. The way I see it, the three main objectives of education should be:

Three objectives of education

1	Preparing students for jobs
2	Preparing students to be responsible citizens
3	Preparing students to appreciate the deeper forms of beauty

preparing students for jobs, preparing students to be responsible citizens and preparing them to be human beings who can enjoy the deeper forms of beauty. The third purpose is as important as the other two, but in truth, the greatest emphasis is on the first purpose, often at the cost or neglect of the other two. As a result of this emphasis on preparing students for jobs, school curriculum in recent years has tilted heavily towards core subjects of language, math, commerce and science. This often leads to a rather one-dimensional growth and development of a student's personality.

Simple creative activities are some of the building blocks of child development and different types of arts play an important role in character building. Learning to create and appreciate visual aesthetics may be more important than ever to the development of the next generation of children as they grow up. While music and theatre have advanced professionally but pursuing other art forms may still not be an economically viable career option for most. Despite the fact that many arts do not offer lucrative career prospects, the truth is, that it is art which makes us more aware of our existence and provides a beautiful and enriching dimension to our life.

Education in arts refers to education in the disciplines of history, literature, social studies, music, dance, theatre and visual arts. Study in the arts is indeed integral to our society. They are a part of our cultural heritage. The arts are what make us most human, most complete as people. The arts cannot be learned through occasional or random exposure any more than math or science can. Education and engagement in the fine arts should be an essential part of the school curriculum and an important component in the educational programme.

Many of the motions involved in making art, such as holding a paintbrush or scribbling with a crayon, are essential to the growth and development of fine motor skills in young children. According to the National Institute of Health, USA, developmental milestones around the age of three years should include drawing a circle and beginning to use safety scissors. Around age four, children should be able to draw a square and begin cutting straight lines with scissors. Many pre-school programmes emphasise the use of scissors because it develops the dexterity children need for writing.

Art is a way to encourage the process and experience of creative thinking

Drawing, sculpting with clay and threading beads on a string and other such activities help develop visual-spatial skills, which today are more important than ever before, for development of the human mind. The fact that toddlers today know how to operate a smartphone even before they can read, means that kids are taking in and reacting to visual information before they can even read or write. This information consists of cues that they get from pictures and books or three-dimensional objects from digital media and television. Parents need to be aware that children today learn a lot more from graphic sources than they did in the past. Children need to know more about the world than just what they can learn through alphabets and numbers. Art education teaches students how to interpret, assimilate and use visual information, and how to make choices based on it. Knowledge about the visual arts, such as graphic symbolism, is especially important in helping kids become smart consumers and navigate a world filled with marketing symbols and logos.

When children are encouraged to express themselves and take risks in creating art, they develop a sense of innovation that will be important in their adult lives. It will help produce the kind of people society needs to take it forward; thinking, inventive, creative people who seek new ways and radical disruptions and not people who can only follow directions. Art is a way to encourage the process and experience of creative thinking.

> *When children are encouraged to express themselves and take risks in creating art they develop a sense of innovation that will help produce the kind of people that society needs to take it forward Thinking, Inventive and Creative*

Steve Jobs, founder of Apple Computers, when launching the iPad2 in 2011, said, "It is in Apple's DNA that technology alone is not enough, it's technology married with liberal arts, married with the humanities, that yields us the results that make our hearts sing."

Planting of trees
is the planting of ideas

Q Sir, I met you at Dehradun many years ago and was touched by your asking the then Defence Minister Shri KC Pant, for a gift of planting 1,00,000 trees around the campus of the Research Centre Imarat. On my numerous visits to project sites in Uttarakhand, Himachal Pradesh and Sikkim, I painfully realised that how felling of trees and construction of roads, a necessity for development, is in a large measure responsible for the increasing ecological imbalance. The sacred pilgrimage spots have been turned into tourist activity areas demanding even more construction of roads and hotels. In countries like China and Korea, highly advanced technology is used for road construction and reinforcing river banks in mountainous areas, so as to minimise the risk from any natural calamity in ecologically fragile areas.

The floods in June 2013 in Uttarakhand would not have been so deadly had the trees covering the Himalayan mountains not been cut so rampantly in the name of development. Indiscriminate felling of trees has made the mountains weak and the topsoil has been washed away, and gone with it is the ability of the soil to absorb the rainwater. The only solution to avoid such disasters is to cover the hills with trees suited to the areas and which have the capacity to absorb water. Trees like that of the walnut, because of their large leaves, are able to absorb more rainwater and control soil erosion. The British planted the fast growing pines which have destroyed the mountains. I urge you to live in Uttarakhand for a year to oversee tree plantation.

Trees are earth's endless effort to speak to the listening heaven
– Rabindranath Tagore

Planting trees in the hills and mountains is the need of the hour. Your suggestion of planting walnut and other appropriate trees to increase the canopy of the forest cover is a practical solution.

The devastating floods in Uttarakhand in 2013 once again draw our attention to the fact that as a nation we have not learnt any lessons from similar tragedies in the past. While the state administration, the Indo-Tibetan Police Force and the armed forces did a commendable job evacuating more than 40,000 people to safer places but 10,000 lives were lost in the disaster. After rescuing people from under the debris of fallen houses, hotels and guest houses, and distributing essentials to survivors, the question is, will the state and central authorities be concerned about rehabilitating the affected communities who are the real victims of the policy of deforestation for development?

I recall the *Chipko Andolan*, the grassroots movement that swept through the Garhwal region in the 1970s, with villagers hugging trees to stop them from being axed. I remember reading what

Sunderlal Bahuguna

the 86-year-old Sunderlal Bahuguna, the leader of *Chipko Andolan*, had said, "The only solution to avoid such disasters is to cover the hills with trees."

During my Presidency, I met Wangari Maathai, the first woman from Kenya to be conferred the Nobel Peace Prize. Wangari Maathai was the first East African woman to receive a PhD in veterinary anatomy. As faculty in the University of Nairobi, she campaigned for equal benefits for the women working on the staff of the University, going so far as to attempt to turn the academic staff association into a union, in order to negotiate for benefits. When ethnic clashes broke out, Maathai travelled throughout Kenya with friends and media persons to areas of violence in order to encourage people to cease fighting. In the 2002 elections, Maathai was elected to the Kenyan Parliament and became a Minister in the Ministry for Environment and Natural Resources.

As a solution for the rising unemployment in Kenya, Maathai fostered the idea of environmental restoration and developed a business that involved the planting of trees to conserve the environment with the involvement of ordinary people. Maathai encouraged the women of Kenya to plant tree nurseries throughout the country, searching nearby forests for seeds to grow trees native to the area. She agreed to pay the women a small stipend for each seedling they brought. Each of these seedlings would be later replanted elsewhere. She started the Green Belt Movement, and focused on planting "trees of peace".

Wangari Maathai

Wangari Maathai was awarded the 2004 Nobel Peace Prize for her 'contribution to sustainable development, democracy and peace', and became the first African woman, and the first environmentalist, to win this prize.

The trees around us are extremely important and have always been critical to human existence and for improving our living environment. We could not exist if there were no trees. A mature leafy tree produces as much oxygen in a season as ten people inhale in a year. What many people do not know is that the forest also acts as a giant filter that purifies the air we breathe. A forest is indeed a carbon storage area or a 'sink' that can lock up as much carbon as it produces. This locking-up process stores carbon as wood and not as a greenhouse gas which pollutes the environment.

Through their roots, trees help to filter the sewage and chemicals, reduce the effects of animal waste, and clean the water runoff into streams. Trees fix nitrates into soil making it more fertile to grow other plants and vegetables. In cities, trees help purify the air by intercepting airborne particles, reducing heat, and absorbing pollutants such as carbon monoxide, sulphur dioxide and nitrogen dioxide. Trees remove these air pollutants by lowering air temperature through respiration, and by retaining particulates.

A mature leafy tree produces as much oxygen in a season as 10 people inhale in a year

Trees act as a giant filter that purify the air we breathe

Trees act as a carbon storage area

Trees are critical to human existence

Let us plant appropriate species of trees on the hill slopes of Uttrakhand and let them grow. If trees are under threat, human life, too, is under threat. Trees are like ideas. Just as we keep pursuing an idea till it turns into reality, in the same way, we should each, plant a tree, and take care of it till it grows to maturity. All of us should commit to planting and protecting at least one tree in our lifetime. This will ensure that there are trees to protect and nourish our future generations.

Empowering women

A full circle
of God's creation

Q As a small-town girl who came to live and work in the city, I believed my life was one of promise. I refused to accept the norms that society around me dictated. It has not been an easy journey and I have faced harassment in all sorts of ways. But despite these experiences, I refuse to give in. I have learned that there are things in life worth fighting for and I will continue to fight for them. There are two sides of India I witness everyday. One, the deeply chauvinistic, unsafe India that often grabs even international media attention, where girls must learn to survive the predators prowling on roads. Two, the beautiful India, which I remember from my childhood days. I want to raise my children here in the city, but with the values with which my parents raised me in our small-town setting. Is that possible?

Sir, would you tell me what types of role models are appropriate for Indian women?

Life shrinks or expands in proportion to one's courage
– Anais Nin

Empowerment of women is at the root of every progressive society. For several centuries in our country there was no focused attention on women and their needs. In fact, they were almost neglected. Many courageous men and women have devoted their entire lives to the cause of betterment of Indian women, so that future generations could be free from the tyranny of inequality and injustice and scale new heights of achievement.

In 1950, a revolutionary change was wrought with equal rights and opportunities to women being enshrined in the Constitution of India. As a result women in independent India are in a comparatively better position today. Some of the problems, which had haunted women for centuries, such as child marriage, practice of 'sati', prohibition of widow remarriage, and discouragement of education for girls, have almost disappeared. Developments in the field of science and technology, access to good education and healthcare, and active socio-political movements have further helped to change the attitude of society towards women. These developments have boosted the morale and self-confidence of women. An increasing number of Indian women now feel that they have their own independent individuality, personality, self-respect, talent, capacity and efficiency. Women who could utilise the opportunities made available to them have proved that they are as capable as men in discharging the responsibilities assigned to them. However, new situations bring with them new challenges. In some ways, as compared to earlier times, the Indian woman today has to bear a heavier burden of managing the home and her career, which is leading to newer stresses and anxieties.

Turning to your question of appropriate role models for women, let me share with you stories of three great women, Marie Curie, Sister Antonia and Madeline De Blic. Marie Curie, was the first woman ever to win a Nobel Prize, the first person to win two Nobel prizes and the only woman, till date, to win it in two fields. Born in Warsaw, in Poland, as Maria Sklodowska, she was a physicist and chemist, who worked mainly in France. She was the first woman professor at the University of Paris. Her achievements include propounding the theory of radioactivity, developing techniques for isolating radioactive isotopes, and the discovery of two elements, polonium and radium. Under her direction, the world's first studies were conducted into the treatment of cancers using radioactive isotopes.

Marie Curie

Maria Sklodowska's family lost their property and wealth in the Polish national uprising, condemning her to a difficult struggle to get ahead in life. She moved to France for higher education where she was barely able to make ends meet on her meagre resources. Braving the harsh cold of the winters without adequate heating and occasionally even fainting from hunger, she continued with her studies.

After graduating in physics, Marie married Pierre Curie and together they worked and conducted research. As the Curies did not have a dedicated laboratory, they conducted most of their research in a shed next to the School of Physics and Chemistry in the University of Paris. The shed, formerly a medical school dissecting room, was poorly ventilated and whenever it rained, the water would leak through the roof. Unaware of the harmful effects of radiation exposure, Marie and Pierre worked with radioactive substances without any protection. In 1903, Marie along with her husband and physicist Henri Becquerel were jointly awarded the Nobel Prize for Physics, for their research on radiation. In 1906, Pierre was killed in a tragic road accident. Despite this personal tragedy, Marie continued with her work and the task of raising her family. In 1911, five years after her husband's death, Marie Curie was once again awarded the Nobel Prize, but this time in the field of chemistry, for her discovery of the elements, radium and polonium.

> *Do not wait for something big to happen Start where you are with whatever you have*

What message can we draw from Marie Curie's life for the women of contemporary India? Do not wait for something big to happen. Start where you are, with whatever you have, and that will lead you to something greater. Begin somewhere because you cannot build a reputation on what you intend to do. You cannot just sit there and wait for people to give you that golden dream, you have got to go out there and make it happen for yourself. Everyone has talent. What is rare is the courage to follow that talent to the place where it leads.

Sometime ago, I was reading a book called, *Everyday Greatness*. I would like to share a story from that book which demonstrates the immense power of a woman. A riot was raging in La Mesa Prison, one of the most notorious prisons in Tijuana in Mexico. Twenty five hundred prisoners were packed into a compound which had been built to accommodate only six hundred. The angry prisoners hurled broken glass bottles at the police who fired back with guns. In this raging battle, suddenly a frail, sixty-eight year old woman,

Sister Antonia

calmly stepped into the crowd. Ignoring the shower of bullets and bottles, this woman, just five feet two inches tall, stood there calmly with outstretched hands in a simple gesture of peace and asked everyone to stop fighting. And incredibly everyone did! No one else in the world, but she could have done this. Her name was Sister Antonia Brenner.

Born as Mary Clarke to a very successful businessman, she was raised in the exclusive and wealthy community of Beverly Hills, California in USA. Despite her privileged lifestyle, she was sensitive to the people's sufferings and would care for those in need around her. Married at a young age, Mary raised seven children in two marriages. Not content with just raising a family, she was also actively involved in charitable activities, along with running her deceased father's business. After twenty-five years of marriage and when most of her children had left home, she drastically changed her life. She sold her home and possessions, became a nun and began to serve the prisoners at La Mesa prison in Tijuana, Mexico.

Why did the prisoners listen to her? They listened because of the decades of her service to the prisoners out of her free choice. She had sacrificed all her comforts for the sake of the prisoners, living in the midst of murderers, thieves and drug peddlers, all of whom she called her sons. She attended to their needs, procured and distributed medicines, counselled the suicidal and washed bodies for the burial. These selfless acts of love and compassion generated respect for Sister Antonia among the prisoners. And on that fateful night in 1994, the prisoners listened to Sister Anotonia and a tragedy, that the riot could have sparked off, was averted.

If women can succeed only by emulating men I think it is a great loss The aim is not only for women to succeed but also to keep their feminine essence and let that influence society

What message does Sister Antonia's life give to the woman of today? Discover your real self, as distinct from your family, as distinct from the man or woman you are in a relationship with. Discover who you are, and what is it that you need to do or to be, to feel good about yourself. Discover the essence of your own self and build upon that. You must be a first grade version of yourself, instead of being a second grade version of somebody else.

If women can succeed only by emulating men, I think it is a great loss and not a success. The aim is not only for women to succeed, but to succeed, while retaining their feminine essence and letting that influence society.

Discover the essence of your own self and build upon it You must be a first grade version of yourself instead of being a second grade version of somebody else

On 8 June 2012, I visited Puducherry to participate in the Golden Jubilee celebrations of Le Volontariat, a non-governmental organisation working for the betterment and upliftment of the deprived sections of the people in Puducherry. When I met the founder of Le Volontariat, Madam Madeleine De Blic, I saw in her the true embodiment of an indomitable spirit. The young Madeleine Herman, as she was known then, came from Belgium to India in 1962 to devote one year of her life to the poorest. Initially she worked in the maternity section of the Cluny Sisters hospital. Then she set up Le Volontariat to help the poor and needy. She married Arnaud de Blic, who had come to India as a teacher at the French Lycée, and never returned. They had two children of their own and adopted two abandoned children.

Over the last five decades, Le Volontariat has empowered a large number of children with education, facilitated the rehabilitation of destitute women and patients afflicted with leprosy, and promoted organic farming in local fields. The Voluntariat offers a kindergarten, an infirmary, evening schools, activity-rooms and serves more than 1600 meals everyday. It also sponsors around 1300 children and has approximately 200 people working for it.

When I look at the service rendered by Le Volontariat, I am reminded of the advice given by Mahatma Gandhi's mother to him when he was nine year old, "Son, in your entire life time if you can save or better someone's life, your birth as a human being and your life is a success. You will have the blessings of the Almighty God."

Madam Madeleine has saved thousands of lives in the last five decades and we are all grateful to her for this unique service. The people lovingly call her 'Amma' or 'Madaleine Amma' and these words of kindness radiate everywhere. When I met her, I saw in her the spirit of service of Mother Teresa and the compassion of Florence Nightingale.

What is the message that we derive from the lives of these three women? A woman is indeed the full circle of God's creation and within her is the power to create, nurture and transform.

The emerging Indian woman of the twenty-first century must be strong in mind, heart, soul and body where strength and spirit, capability and compassion go together.

The great poet, Subramanya Bharathi (1882-1921) composed the poem, "Envisioning Women of India", which beautifully highlights the profile of the emerging woman:

Emerging woman
She walks with raised head
with her eyes looking straight
She has her principles
unafraid of anybody
She has a lofty
and knowledge based pride
Such cultured women
don't falter from the chosen path
She drives ignorance away
She welcomes the bliss of life
with learned mind
This is the Dharma
of the emerging woman

Clutches of discrimination

Q Sir, on the one hand we see women entering all kinds of professions, holding senior positions in large corporations, becoming engineers, doctors, managers and political leaders. But we also see that there is a simultaneous and continuous rise in the graph of crimes against women. How do you explain this apparent contradiction?

I live in Delhi, where as compared to other cities, women enjoy more freedom. But that does not reflect the reality in terms of the inequality between women and men. Women do not get the same respect that their male counterparts get in the workplace. No matter what status a woman may achieve outside home, inside the home she, by and large, remains a chattel. When this is the ground reality of the women at home and at the workplace, it is clear that despite receiving education and attaining financial independence, their status vis-à-vis the status of men is still far from that of equality.

My personal view is that the rise of women in society and the crime against women going hand-in-hand is not difficult to understand. It is clear that men would obviously not like to give up their importance or even share it with women. It is the men who resent the rise of women, and before women can rise to unchallengeable heights, the ogre in man wants to crush them.

Sir, why do you think this peculiar situation persists and how can we correct it?

The sense of discrimination between oneself and others is delusion. Treating females as inferior is the worst form of delusion
– APJ Abdul Kalam

From enjoying equal status with men in ancient times, through the low points of the medieval period, to the promotion of equal rights by many reformers, the history of women in India has been eventful. Although the Constitution of India grants men and women equal rights but in reality great gender disparities remain. Violence against women is the most pervasive expression of this gender-based discrimination and remains widespread. According to a global poll conducted by The Thomson Reuters Foundation and published in *India Today* (June 16, 2011), India is the 'fourth most dangerous country' in the world for women, and the worst country for women among the G20 countries. In this poll, experts from across the world were asked to rank countries on the basis of their perception of overall danger and six specific parameters: health threats; sexual violence; non-sexual violence; harmful practices rooted in culture, tradition and religion; lack of access to economic resources; and human trafficking. It is an extremely sad reflection of the 'progress' that we Indians so proudly talk about when half the population of our country is deprived of its basic rights, including the very basic right to life.

Amongst all countries of the world India is ranked the fourth most dangerous country for women Among the G20 countries India is ranked as the worst for women

This survey reflects that lack of education and access to healthcare are as deadly, if not more so, than physical dangers like rape and murder which usually grab the headlines. In the five countries considered most dangerous for women (and this includes India), basic human rights are systematically denied to women. Women continue to have little say over their lives. They have practically no access to finances, land, inheritance rights, education, employment, justice, healthcare and nutrition.

I discussed this issue with many experts and two major reasons emerge for this. First, is the sad fact that in India, girls are valued less than boys. This value-distortion results in many inequalities in society. In addition to rampant sex-selective abortions, there are significant disparities in access to healthcare and education. The second is the prevalence of a culture of complicity. There is not enough exposure and conviction against those who are perpetrating acts of violence against women. There are innumerable cases where police officers pressurise victims to keep silent or even marry their own rapists to avoid prosecution.

But the widespread anger which erupted in the aftermath of the Nirbhaya rape case in Delhi in December 2012 seems to indicate that there is an opportunity for change and could, in fact, result in some substantive changes for women. It is not enough to merely have laws, the implementation needs to be resourced well enough for the laws to be effective. There are indications that this could happen in the near future.

Lack of access to education and healthcare are as deadly if not more so than physical dangers like rape and murder which usually grab the headlines

India's economic liberalisation, which began in the early nineties, has helped the nation achieve near double-digit growth over the last five years, making it Asia's third largest economy after China and Japan. The rapid emergence of the corporate sector and the spread of higher education amongst girls has meant that more women, than ever before, are taking up professional positions. But despite their professional success, in most Indian households, it is the woman who is expected to look after the home and the children and also manage the cooking and cleaning. Their families, as a result, often view their professional jobs as a means of income, rather than as a career. As a result of such

Violence against women is the most pervasive expression of gender-based discrimination and remains widespread

pressures, there is a prevailing mindset that women are less committed to work and end up compromising their work for their home life.

I feel there is urgent need for systemic change to bring in greater diversity in the workplace and encourage competent women to overcome the hurdles that society places in their career path. This is the time we should boldly implement steps to actually make women and men equal.

Education holds the key to women empowerment Education not only of women but also of those who think that they are superior to women

The Women's Quota Bill has been introduced in the Lok Sabha at least half a dozen times, but it has not yet been enacted. In spite of attempts by many political parties to increase the representation of women in their parties, the number remains far below the desired target. Personally, I am for at least 33 per cent reservation for women in all legislative bodies including the Parliament. This will help the next generation of young women in our country to be more assured and self-confident.

Women have enormous potential that can be used in the process of development and nation-building. Education holds the key to this, and education not only of women, but also of all those persons who think that they are superior to women.

A chilling reality

Q Sir, in India the girl child has been a topic of discussion and debate for the past several decades but, sadly even today, her position in society remains rather deplorable. The girl was always an unwanted child and was often killed at birth. With the advancement of science and technology this killing has gone still further, and the girl child is now being killed even before birth! Such a scenario does not augur well for the future of women in our society. I read the speech you gave at the 7th Civil Service Day and liked your idea of innovative leadership to combat social evils. You give hope but, in reality, no one single factor, be it education, profession, legal rights or even the combination of all these, can result in a solution. The only feasible solution is a change of mindset, a change of attitude of the men towards women.

Tell me, Sir, how can this be done? Will you take

a lead? Till this is done, no amount of teaching, preaching or legislation will help the girl child.

Killing unborn daughters is a sin against life. It consists perhaps not so much in despairing of life, as in hoping for another life and in eluding the implacable grandeur of this life
– APJ Abdul Kalam

Female foeticide is not a new phenomenon in India, but has reached widespread proportions in recent decades. It is sad that a positive scientific development meant for a good cause is being misused to kill off baby girls while still in their mothers' wombs.

Amniocentesis was first started in India in 1974 as part of a sample survey conducted at the All India Institute of Medial Sciences (AIIMS), New Delhi, to detect fetal abnormalities. These tests were later stopped by the Indian Council of Medical Research (ICMR), but by then their potential commercial value had leaked out, and 1979 saw the first sex determination clinic opening in Amritsar in Punjab. Women organisations across the country tried their best to put a stop to this new menace, but they were helpless as the Medical Termination of Pregnancy (MTP) Act 1971 permitted the use of the amniocentesis test for detecting foetal abnormalities. According to the MTP Act, any abnormality detected between twelve to eighteen weeks of gestational period in the foetus, provides legal grounds for an abortion which can be carried out up to the twentieth week of pregnancy. Because of this provision, amniocentesis could not be banned and its gross misuse for detecting a girl child, rather than any abnormality in the foetus, continues un- checked.

Female foeticide in India is no longer only an issue of violation of women's rights but rather it has become a social malaise.

According to the United Nations an estimated 2,000 unborn girls are illegally aborted every day in India

According to the United Nations, an estimated 2,000 unborn girls are illegally aborted every day in India. This is reflected in the demographic profile of India where according to the Census of India 2011 there were 940 women for every 1000 men, that is 60 women less for every 1000 members of the population. A more detailed analysis reveals that states such as Kerela and Puducherry have the best sex-ratios while a state such as Haryana has the worst sex-ratio. The fact that Kerela has the highest literacy rates amongst states in India and the best sex-ratio, a direct linkage between the two can be assumed.

India needs to urgently address on a war footing the problem of female foeticide which continues unabated despite the spread of education

It is unfortunate, that despite the spread of education there has been little or no change in the psychology and heartless behaviour of the people who cause death of the vulnerable female foetus. The Pre- Conception and Pre-Natal Diagnostic Techniques (PCPNDT) Act, enacted first in 1994, and amended thrice since then, has not been successful in curbing this menace. On the contrary, it has contributed to the mushrooming growth of private clinics all over the country which people desperately visit for conducting sex selective abortions. The fact that female foeticide continues unabated indicates that it is one of the gravest challenges of the twenty-first century which India needs to effectively tackle. If not, it is bound to give rise to serious social problems. After all, just as a bird cannot fly on one wing, nature cannot survive on the shoulders of disproportional men alone. For the growth and development of mankind and the progress of humanity, men and women cannot be in conflict with one another; rather they are sought to be in coordination and cooperation with one another. Saving the girl child is absolutely imperative for the future of the human race.

Let me share a Biblical story with you. The story revolves around the question: Why did God create woman from man's rib, when He could have simply created her from dust, as He created man?

Just as a bird cannot fly on one wing nature cannot survive without balance between men and women

God said to the first woman, "When I created the heavens and the earth, I spoke them into being. When I created man, I formed him from the dust of the earth and breathed life into his nostrils. After I breathed the breath of life into man, I allowed a deep sleep to come over him so I could patiently and perfectly fashion you. Man was put to sleep so that he could not interfere with my creativity. I fashioned you from one of man's bones. I chose the bone that protects man's life. I chose the rib, which protects his heart and lungs, and supports him, as you are meant to do.

Around this one bone, I shaped and modelled you. I created you perfectly and beautifully. Your characteristics are as the rib, strong yet delicate and fragile. You provide protection for the most delicate organ in man, his heart. His heart is the centre of his being; his lungs hold the breath of life. The rib cage will allow itself to be broken before it will allow damage to the heart. You will support man as the rib cage supports the heart.

You were not taken from man's feet, to be under him, nor were you taken from his head, to be above him. You were taken from his side, to stand beside him and to be held close to his side. You are my perfect angel. You are my beautiful little girl. You have grown

For growth and development of mankind and progress of humanity men and women cannot be in conflict with one another rather they are sought to be in coordination and cooperation with one another

to be a splendid woman of excellence, and my eyes fill with pride when I see the virtue in your heart. Your eyes are full of beauty. Your lips, how lovely when they part in prayer. Your nose is so perfect in form, your hands are so gentle to touch. I have caressed your face in your deepest sleep, I've held your heart close to mine. Of all that lives and breathes, you are the most like me.

Adam walked with me in the cool of the day and yet he was lonely. He could not see me or touch me. He could only feel me. So everything I wanted Adam to share and experience with me, I fashioned in you: my holiness, my strength, my purity, my love, my protection and support. You are special because you are the extension of me. Man represents my image, woman represents my emotions. Together, you both represent the totality of God.

Then God commanded the first Man: treat Woman well. Love her, respect her, for she is fragile. In hurting her, you hurt me. What you do to her, you do to me. In crushing her, you only damage your own heart, the heart of your Father."

God created man and woman as equals. To disrespect or harm a woman is to disrespect God.

Paradise is
at the feet of mother

Q Tears rolled down my cheeks as I heard your lecture, 'Smiling mother family'. I recently lost my mother to breast cancer which could not be diagnosed in time. Though I miss her very much, her departure brought with it this great realisation which I want to share with you.

Most men, like myself, go through life very comfortably, without being conscious of the innumerable 24x7 tasks our mothers are always involved in; raising children, taking care of the household and even managing their careers. Many of us still enjoy the privileges and legacy of our male-dominated cultural norms and practices. If we seriously observe and account the daily tasks and responsibilities of mothers, they are many and varied, as compared with those of fathers, especially when it comes to the unparalleled obligation and challenge of raising decent children. Men think that a father's role is only that of a provider and consequently struggle with their role as a parent.

Married women with young children work more hours, ranging from fourteen to sixteen hours per day, as compared to married men who work not more than eight to ten hours a day. And in households where women are the sole breadwinners, the burden they carry is unimaginably heavier.

Sir, my blood boils whenever I read about the harassment that women have to undergo in our society. How can these men who assault, attack and misbehave with women, forget that they came into this world through a woman. I request you to tell me what I can do to make our society safer for women.

My mother was the most beautiful woman I ever saw. All I am I owe to my mother. I attribute all my success in life to the moral, intellectual and physical education I received from her
– George Washington

I share your concern about the male-dominated cultural norms and practices which we still seem to be stuck with in our society. This is despite the fact that the Constitution of India guarantees equality to women as a fundamental right. Notwithstanding that, the way women are regarded and treated is an indicator of the low worth placed on the feminine within human societies. The implication of this is, at the very least, discriminatory and at the worst, threatens our very existence.

The life-giving, life-preserving, the nurturing, the emotional, the compassionate, the sharing, the deep, the feminine energy has been systematically neglected, belittled, bashed, humiliated, mutilated, tortured, hunted and killed by the male principle that has taken over our thinking and behaviour at every level in society. It is time to value emotions such as love and compassion and encourage behaviour that leads to sharing, caring and peaceful living.

A woman is indeed the full circle of God's creation and within her is the power to Create, Nurture and Transform

I recently came upon a poem titled, "Just One" written by an unknown author which is:

> One song can spark a moment
> One flower can wake the dream
> One tree can start a forest
> One bird can herald spring
>
> One smile begins a friendship
> One handclasp lifts a soul
> One star can guide a ship at sea
> One word can frame the goal
>
> One vote can change a nation
> One sunbeam lights a room
> One candle wipes out darkness
> One laugh will conquer gloom

One step must start each journey
One word must start each prayer
One hope will raise our spirits
One touch can show you care

One voice can speak with wisdom
One heart can know what's true

One life can make a difference
And that life can be you!

Just as 'one life can make a difference', this realisation of the true worth of your mother should become the starting point to make a difference in the lives of all the mothers around you, whether in the homes of your relatives, friends, neighbours, colleagues. Share this realisation with all the people around you, and let it be manifest in your changed behaviour. Only when each one of us makes the change can we change society, because society is nothing but an aggregation of individuals. If each individual changes, society too will change.

Reading your mail reminded me of the days of World War II, when I was ten years old and living with my family in Rameswaram. There was scarcity of most food items and articles of daily use. Ours was a large joint family with five sons and five daughters, three of whom had their own families. My mother would be up at four every morning, then wake me up, help me bathe and get dressed to go to my teacher, Shri Swamiyar, for learning mathematics. I would return home from tuition at five-thirty and my father would be waiting to take me to the Arabic school to learn *Namaz* and the holy *Quran Sharif*. After that I would go to the Rameswaram Road railway station, located three kilometers away, to collect a bundle of newspapers thrown out from the passing

Madras-Dhanushkodi Express. I would pick up the bundle and run around Rameswaram distributing newspapers in the town. By the time I would reach home after distributing the newspapers, it would be eight o'clock and my mother would give me a breakfast comprising of a special quota compared to my other brothers and sisters as I was simultaneously studying and working. In the evening, after school, again I would go around Rameswaran to collect dues from the customers to whom I had delivered the newspaper in the morning.

One day, as all of us were sitting and eating, my mother kept giving me one *chapati* after the other, and hungry as I was, I continued eating. When I finished eating, my elder brother called me aside and scolded me saying, "Kalam, do you know what was happening? You went on eating *chapatis* and mother went on giving you. She gave you her share of *chapatis* too, and now there are none left for her. These are very difficult times. Be a responsible son and do not make your mother starve." I had this shivering sensation and unable to control myself I rushed to my mother and hugged her.

Realisation of the true worth of your mother should become the starting point to make a difference in the lives of all the mothers around you Let this realisation be manifest in your changed behaviour Only when each one of us changes can we change society because society is nothing but the aggregation of individuals

My mother lived for ninety-three years. She was full of love and kindness, and above all a woman of divine nature, who performed the *Namaz* five times everyday. She looked angelic in prayer and seeing her I would be inspired and moved.

Just as we need to love and respect our mothers, we also need to realise that Mother Earth, the entity that has given birth to all life and which sustains us, has been exploited to a point where we can no longer count on her rapidly depleting resources for our future sustenance. Instead of following the principles of preservation and sustainability, we seem to have almost solely adopted the masculine principles of exploitation. If we want to sustain this planet and if humankind wants to evolve rather than regress, we need to urgently begin to redress the balance by exploring the feminine, its characteristics, its qualities and its way of thinking. We need to value and cultivate the underlying qualities of behaviour that aim to preserve life, share resources, negotiate and compromise, increase love and compassion, or in other words, to evolve, we need to manifest the feminine aspects of creation within human society.

> *If we want to sustain this planet and if humankind wants to evolve rather than regress we need to urgently begin to redress the imbalance by exploring the feminine and its characteristics its qualities and its way of thinking*

Inspired by my mother, I wrote a poem titled, "My Mother" which I would like to share with you:

> I still remember the day when I was ten
> Sleeping on your lap to the envy of
> my elder brothers and sisters
> It was full moon night, my world only
> you knew Mother! My Mother!
> When at midnight, I woke with tears
> falling on my knee
> You knew the pain of your child, my Mother
> Your caring hands, tenderly removing the pain
> Your love, your care, your faith gave me strength
> To face the world without fear and with His strength
> We will meet again on the great Judgment Day
> My Mother!

Building
a strong India

Grooming
leaders for tomorrow

Q Most Indian corporate leaders greatly cherish the crown of the top job as is evident from the fact that many who have crossed their seventieth birthday are still at the helm of affairs. They are either slogging to find a successor or persuading their companies to extend the retirement age saying they have still not applied their mind to succession planning. These leaders find the prospect of relinquishing their job downright depressing. For them, leaving their position means failure or professional death. They love the job and the position as it is their only identity. They think of building a cohort of potential leaders, not as the path to growth and prosperity, but as a route to maintaining a lame-duck status within the organisation.

Sir, at **ISRO** and **DRDO**, you had proved, that careful succession planning can groom people internally. Insiders who know the culture, the people, and the nuances of their competitors are able to lead the organisation on to greater success. Many of your juniors whom you trained are now heading large projects and organisations.

In politics, it is mostly family members who are promoted as leaders. Nearly 40 per cent of the Members of Parliament of the Congress party reached there through a family connection, more than 10 per cent of the other political parties are also following the same route. Why are you hesitating in highlighting this important aspect of institutional building? You are the only person who can say this truth and be heard.

Until an organisation becomes intentional about development of internal talent, it is doomed to an ever-growing leadership deficit
−APJ Abdul Kalam

Your mail put me in a reflective mood. I spent twenty years at the Indian Space Research Organisation (ISRO) and another twenty at the Defence Research and Development Organisation (DRDO). During this long period of time, I nurtured and groomed many young professionals into team leaders. A few of them went on to become leaders of large national programmes. Some of my distinguished colleagues include Madhavan Nair, Chairman ISRO, Kota Harinarayana, Chief of Light Combat Aircraft programme, VK Saraswat and Avinash Chander, Chief of DRDO and A. Sivathanu

Pillai, Chief of BrahMos, and Dr Prahlada, Vice-Chancellor of the Defence Institute of Advanced Technology. There are many others who are heading national laboratories and large companies. When I look back at the growth of these leaders, I can identify seven distinct processes needed for building leadership capacity.

These seven processes are applicable to any organisation. But the time, effort and resources needed to pursue each process and the complexity of any or all the processes would vary depending on the organisation's size, ownership, mission, individual characteristics and needs.

The first process is the engagement of senior leaders. As with any strategic priority, effective leadership development begins with the active commitment and engagement of senior leaders. They will define the priority for this task of leadership grooming and allocate resources for it. These senior leaders need to own this initiative and must actively dedicate time and resources to the effort. Similarly, line managers must be equipped and held accountable for developing future leaders. I have seen how VS Arunchalam worked to get me funding for the Integrated Guided Missile Programme. Later Kota Harinarayana and Sivathanu Pillai worked tirelessly to mobilise funding for the Light Combat Aircraft and BrahMos respectively. Without the active backing and involvement of the top leaders, no programme of leadership development can be successful.

The second process is acquiring an understanding about the future needs of the organisation. This very essential step in building a leadership pipeline entails mapping out the kinds of roles, skills, and numbers the organisation will need in the future to achieve its strategic goals.

The third process is assessing the potential of the current employees to fulfil the future roles needed in the organisation. This is sometimes referred to as, identifying 'high-potential employees' or 'succession candidates'. The actual process of identifying these future leaders can be challenging, as current leaders will need to think about how to map backwards from future

	Processes
1	Engagement of senior leaders
2	Understanding the future needs of the organisation
3	Identifying 'high-potential' employees
4	Development & mentoring of identified 'high-potential' employees
5	Inducting leaders from the external eco-system, if needed
6	Measurement & improvement of practices
7	Building a culture that supports leadership development

Processes needed for building leadership capacity

strategic needs, to the skills an individual currently demonstrates, and determine how to define and identify 'potential'.

The fourth process is the actual development and mentoring of the identified 'high-potential employees'. In addition to commitment from employees and their managers, helping the identified staff achieve their full potential is likely to require a variety of support including, but not limited to, formal training. Most important are on-the-job 'stretch' opportunities, for example, temporary projects or role assignments, and mentoring and coaching from line managers or other senior leaders within the organisation. For instance, Arun Tiwari developed a titanium air bottle for the TRISHUL Missile System while working with Dr G J Gururaja at Bharat Heavy Plates and Vessels Ltd at Vishakapatnam.

The fifth process is of inducting leaders from the external eco-system, if needed. The number of internal promotions versus external inductions is likely to vary from organisation to organisation. For positions that cannot be developed internally, organisations will need to put in place practices to source, attract, screen and integrate the external hires. Screening for cultural fit is perhaps the most difficult yet essential part of this process, and must remain an emphasis during the integration of the external inductees. In 1988, I invited Prof G Venkatraman to set up the Advanced Numerical Research & Analysis Group in DRDO and brought in Sivathanu Pillai from ISRO to manage the Missile Programme.

The sixth process is to measure and improve practices. As with any core process within an organisation, senior leaders should continuously step back to assess the effectiveness of the organisation's leadership development processes. This includes refining the processes based on results achieved. Sometimes it becomes necessary to modify the practices, especially if there is any change in strategic priorities. The organisation that can track the impact of its capacity-building efforts is more likely to get

Leadership position maybe inherited but leadership capacity cannot be inherited It has to be built

the commitment and resources required from internal and external sources. We had created a very competent Computation Fluid Dynamics at DRDO working against the formidable Missile Technology Control Regime (MTCR) which essentially was a ganging up of 34 countries to prevent the proliferation of missile and unmanned aerial vehicle technology capable of carrying a 500 kilograms payload upto 300 kilometres.

The seventh process, and which is the most difficult to implement, is that of building a culture that supports leadership development. Changing the status quo is the toughest task for any leader. Successful organisations make leadership development an intentional part of the culture. When a culture of feedback and professional development is fostered openly and intentionally with all the employees, the organisation is better able to develop leaders and inspire the employees to stay engaged. Senior leaders should create an environment in which employees can express interest in leadership positions and feel supported in their development, and those who invest in them feel recognised for their efforts.

To answer your specific query on succession of political leadership, if the young successors are not competent and well groomed, there will be disastrous consequences. While the leadership position maybe inherited but leadership capacity has to be built, it cannot be inherited.

A nation is
built through sacrifice

Q Sir, I am in deep sorrow after hearing the
news of the sinking of our submarine INS
Sindhurakshak. My father works in the Indian Navy
and I was there at the shore when you visited
Visakhapatnam in February 2006, and went on board
the INS Sindhurakshak submarine. I am sure you
would remember some of the Naval officers you
met when the submarine dived and sailed in the
Bay of Bengal for a few hours.

As a child, I thought these submarines were
absolutely magical. I would wonder how a ship
that sinks, can come back up on to the surface
and then again sink to the bottom? My father would
try to explain how the submarine sucks up water
and sinks to the bottom of the seabed, and then
releases that water to come back up on to the
surface. I would nod, pretending that I had

understood, but I don't think I have quite grasped it to this day. And then, I recall the time my father would be on duty, sailing for weeks and sometimes for months on end. As kids we were used to this and thought of it as routine, completely and totally oblivious of the risks involved. To this day, I remember how anxious my mother would be when dad would go sailing. On the days she knew he was going to be above ground, she would sleep a little more peacefully. To her, when the submarine was docked in a harbour, even if she didn't know which one, it meant everything was fine, it was a 'safe' day. And then there were the anxious days, when he would be sailing. Those days were spent watching the calendar trying to guess where he would be, and waiting for that one welcome phone call from dad to say that everything was okay. If that phone call was delayed by a day or two, my mother would be worried and anxious.

Eighteen of our brave sailors will never emerge out of the deep waters where INS Sindhurakshak sank. What makes it even sadder is that this happened when the submarine was docked in the Naval Dockyard. It happened on a 'safe' day. I find it easy to empathise with the families of the crew killed on board. It could have been my family.

I read a newspaper report that a team of Russian experts which visited the Naval Dockyard after the sinking of INS Sindhurakshak had suggested that the tragedy might have been set off by 'mishandling of equipment'. Some other newspaper stories suggest that two blasts tore through the vessel and started a blaze that ignited some weapons on board. This generated fierce temperatures that melted parts of the internal hull and deformed hatches. I find both these theories insulting. May I ask you, Dr Kalam, what are your thoughts on this submarine tragedy?

The law of sacrifice is uniform throughout the world. To be effective, it demands the sacrifice of the bravest and the most spotless
– Mahatma Gandhi

I felt extreme anguish and sadness when I heard about the sinking of the INS Sindhurakshak on 14 August 2013 and the death of its eighteen crew personnel.

I had sailed with INS Sindhurakshak for a day on 13 February 2006 and learnt about the intricacies of submarine operations. We travelled about five miles off the coast of Visakhapatnam and went down to a depth of 50 metres. Commander Pravesh Singh Bisht explained the functioning of the submarine and took me around the five compartments of the boat. He explained that INS Sindhurakshak was the 9th in the series of Kilo Class submarines of the Indian Navy. Commissioned on 24 December 1997 at St Petersburg, Russia, INS Sindhurakshak had already taken part in two military conflicts in 1999 and in 2002.

It was reported that as two explosions rocked the submarine, a huge ball of fire escaped from the conning tower hatch, the only hatch that is left open when a submarine is in the harbour. Since the flames came out of the conning tower hatch nobody in these areas could have survived. As I heard this sad news I recollected the harrowing tragedy of the HS-748 Avro disaster on 11 January 1999, in which eight personnel were killed. The Avro, which belonged to the Defence Research and Development Organisation (DRDO), was a test platform for developing a sophisticated indigenous Airborne Early Warning (AEW) system.

Officers must be assured that the fault lines can be identified and set right so that they can continue working in the highly demanding missions with full confidence

In cases of such incidents it is very easy to jump to conclusions and expound some pet theories. Sabotage, problems with the modifications, hydrogen explosion or a handling accident that set off the chain of events are some of the theories in circulation; the most tempting of these being the sabotage theory because that makes the incident an open-and-shut case. We should not fall for or be distracted by such theories. To find the truth, the Indian Navy needs to determine for itself, not only the cause of this incident, but also to put in place procedures and precautions that would ensure such incidents never recur. Sailors and naval officers must be assured that the fault lines can be identified and set right so that they continue working in the highly demanding missions that are conducted in the submarines, with the fullest confidence.

From the information made available, it seems the submarine was being prepared for an operational deployment and was expected to sail in the early morning. The entire crew was scheduled to arrive on board at about 0300 hours to prepare the submarine for sea. The full outfit of eighteen weapons in this type of submarine consists of a mixture of missiles, oxygen torpedoes and electric torpedoes. Of these, six are stowed in the tubes and twelve on racks in the torpedo compartment. Normally, weapons kept on the racks are not 'armed'. This means that the mechanisms and devices required to detonate the high explosives in the warheads are not placed inside them, thus rendering them safe.

Taking into consideration that only two explosions were heard, it would mean that the remaining sixteen warheads, each containing approximately 250 kilograms of high explosives did not explode. This indicates that the inherent stability and safety of the warhead's design played a vital role in mitigating collateral damage.

Life is a very complex interplay of various factors and there has to be acceptance of the risks inherent in coping with it and yet keep moving on

What worries me is that had the accident occurred when the submarine was out at sea, the death toll would have been devastating and there would have been no chance of salvaging any part of it. The Deep Submergence Rescue Vehicle programme has to be in place because, both, safeguarding personnel integrity and India's war preparedness, are very essential.

We pass through this world but once and nothing can be more tragic than the sudden stunting of young lives. When such accidents occur, we are confronted with the reality that despite our having tamed and harnessed many of nature's forces, sometimes situations do become catastrophic when machines get out of control or they malfunction. Every time an airline pilot takes off with hundreds of passengers on board, he not only relies on his own skills as a pilot, but also on the competence of the engineers who built the aircraft, the navigators who keep the aircraft on course and the ground staff who provide support for a safe landing. But beyond all these man-managed factors, there is always the unpredictable factor of weather, air turbulence and even the possibility of sabotage. So, indeed, life is a very complex interplay of various factors and there has to be acceptance of the risks inherent in coping with it and yet keep moving on.

Unity of mind and heart

Q Sir, I was born in 1994 in Ayodhya. Yesterday you had come to KS Saket Post Graduate College in Ayodhya. I tried to meet you but was prevented by zealous volunteers of the event and the police. You asked us, young students, to reflect upon what we would like to be remembered for? Let me share with you my own small perspective.

Ayodhya is a quiet medieval city of spires and domes reflecting ancient Hindu temple architecture with a dash of Mughal style. The Sarayu river which flanks the city is forlorn, waiting for pilgrims. The streets and the bazaars of the city are empty. Vendors, with their brassware idols and local sweets such as *besan laddoos, pedas, jalebis,* seemingly untouched by the homogenising flood of globalisation, sit patiently, waiting for buyers.

The guarded site of the Babri Masjid-Ram Janambhoomi is generally quiet and bereft of visitors. The sandstone blocks and the pillars, meant for the Ram Temple are piled up in large stacks, their pink colour darkened by thick layers of dust and moss. I fear that someday, suddenly, people from outside Ayodhya will descend here and the conflict will again start. Why don't we build something here that belongs to the entire humanity and not to any one religion? Are not different religions made by man? And is it not true that there is only one God? If so, then why do these clashes keep happening?

Even if a unity of faith is not possible, a unity of love is
– Hans Urs von Balthasar

My dear young friend, I indeed enjoyed my visit to KS Saket Post Graduate College at Ayodhya. There were so many young students, probably thousands of them. It is a pity that you could not meet me and I must make up for it by writing you this mail.

Your fear, that suddenly people from outside will gather in Ayodhya and again start a conflict, is not totally irrational as we have seen such things happening in the past. But I must tell you that there is hope. The youth have seen through the danger of raking up conflicts buried in the past. The orientation must turn around from the past to the future and focus on how India can become a developed nation. The real issue is that we are not able to see ourselves as a nation and because of that there is no national vision.

During my Presidency, I met a group of freedom fighters at the Rashtrapati Bhawan. Each one of them constituted the life-force of our freedom movement. I saluted them as they had fought for our freedom and sacrificed their comforts to achieve our Independence. The seeding of this great vision to achieve India's freedom took place in 1857. For ninety years after that there were a number of intensive struggles for freedom. Many of our people and leaders were in jail for long periods and their sufferings got transformed into the struggle for freedom under the leadership of Mahatma Gandhi. In my discussion with the group, I tried to recapture the essence of the freedom movement. Two distinct points emerged: the first, that we got our Independence as a result of the supreme sacrifices, dedication and focused efforts of the people; the second, that the vision-driven movement created many leaders in different spheres of politics, economics, industry, science, arts and culture. After Independence, these different sectoral leaders helped India make significant achievements in agriculture and food production, energy, healthcare, education and various fields of science and technology; and in the international arena in the fields of pharmaceuticals, information technology, mass media and communication, space, defence and nuclear science.

The issue is that we are not able to see ourselves as a nation and because of that there is no national vision

Similar to this first vision, which created a movement to achieve freedom with unity of minds of our people and the unity of purpose in actions, we now need a second national vision which would integrate people from all walks of our society towards a common purpose. The second vision of our nation would transform it from the present status of a developing to a developed nation by integrated actions simultaneously in the areas of agriculture and food processing, education and healthcare, infrastructure development including power, information and communication technologies, and critical technologies. This great vision will aim to alleviate poverty, illiteracy and unemployment. When the minds of our citizens are unified and focused towards this vision, the dormant potential will manifest as a mammoth power leading to a happy and prosperous life for a billion people. This vision of the nation will also remove the conflicts arising out of differences and small thinking.

I will now address your fear of recurring clashes at Ayodhya. Ayodhya is a divine land enriched with the faith of two religions, both of which have been the cornerstones of human civilization. It represents the cradle of human history and its timeless struggles and triumphs. I visualise the holy land of Ayodhya emerging as an unblemished symbol of humanity's quest for service and a beacon of the nation's spirit of harmonious integrity by the year 2020. I envisage Ayodhya to be a Humanity Healing Centre, the founding place for a state-of-the-art multi-dimensional healing centre, a place which alleviates pains of all forms: physical, mental and spiritual. This healing centre should have four essential features.

First, it should develop as a low-cost healthcare centre for all age groups. It should be the home for the best health services, especially for the poor and elderly of the nation. It should operate on the pattern, already existing in several hospitals in India, where almost

70 per cent patients are treated free. It should be a place where hundreds of doctors are dedicated to restore vision to a million visually-impaired every year, where multi-dimensional experts give mobility to the handicapped and hope to those in abject despair. It should be a centre where modern medicine finds confluence with the traditional medical systems of Ayurveda, Unani, Siddha, Naturopathy and Yoga to heal the body and deliver compassionate healthcare to the needy.

Vision for Ayodhya as a Human Healing Centre

A low-cost healthcare centre	A centre of excellence for quality research
Amalgamation of physical and spiritual healing	A centre for imparting value based knowledge

Second, it should emerge as a centre of excellence for quality research which generates technological solutions for national health problems. Even as we are emerging as the fourth largest economy in the world (in terms of purchasing power parity), every second child born in the nation is malnourished and 53 out every 1000 infants do not live to celebrate their first birthday. Almost half of the worldwide tuberculosis patients are Indians. Anemic levels in Indian women are amongst the highest in the world. Availability of clean water and nutritious food still remains the foremost lack in the lives of millions of Indians. The Humanity Healing Centre should focus on how such stark realities, which are amongst the most prominent national concerns, can be addressed in an effective, pervasive and cost-efficient manner to reach the remote rural sectors of the nation. It should be a Centre which, in collaboration with international agencies, researches low cost preventive vaccine development for diseases which have plagued humanity for ages.

Third, the Humanity Healing Centre should accentuate the amalgamation of the physical with spiritual healing. It should emerge as a multi-religious spiritual platform, with lush green surroundings vibrating with colourful flowers and melodious birds. With its proximity to multiple rich religions, the Healing Centre would derive the best out of all faiths, and use it as a therapy to treat ailing souls. It would thus be a place of spiritual learning where people would find proximity with the divinity and the conscience of the human soul shall awaken.

The Centre would be a place where ideas are not bound by the shackles of any religion and where creativity is unleashed for national transformation

The fourth pillar of the Humanity Healing Centre should be based on the foundation of imparting value-based knowledge to people from around the world. It would be a crucible for confluence of diverse faiths which would facilitate the youth to imbibe and adhere to values which the nation would be proud of. The question is, can different religions converge at Ayodhya, and lead to the creation of a society which is free from corruption and moral turpitude?

The Humanity Healing Centre would be a place where the best moral education syllabus would be researched across the spectrum of multiple religions and which would use the most efficient methodology for its delivery.

Who will create such a Centre? The government and private sector should support the development of the Centre which would be a symbol of healing to humanity regardless of their colour, religion, caste, gender or nationality. Specifically, I propose the Centre to be jointly created, owned and operated in the public-private-community partnership mode with the government, all political parties and organisations joining it, along with professionals from different fields, retired servicemen and scholars from all communities.

Creation of the Humanity Healing Centre at Ayodhya would be a colossal step to shed the bitter pangs of the past hostilities and create a future based on our aspirations which all humanity shall cherish and be inspired by

Thus, we see Ayodhya, in another decade, to be the world's renowned place for evolution of enlightened citizenship. A place where value-based education is imparted and where multiple religions converge along with their shared spirituality. It would be a place where ideas are not bound by the shackles of any religion and where creativity is unleashed for national transformation.

Thus transformed, Ayodhya will have a significant impact on the future of the nation and its one billion people. Today, it stands as a defining moment, with consequences which have had far reaching effects. It is our great opportunity today to take actions, based on our aspirations of the future, rather than letting it be governed by the baggage of differences from the past. Our future generations will revere us for taking an action which will help humanity and not that which will destroy harmony and peace. It is the golden opportunity for this generation, to be remembered as harbingers of lasting fraternity and enlightened nationhood rather than generators of thousand year conflicts. A resolution to create the Humanity Healing Centre at Ayodhya would be a colossal step to shed the bitter pangs of the past hostilities and create a future which all nations and humanity shall cherish and be inspired by.

Nurturing the roots

Q Sir, I heard your speech on the User Community Pyramid. The movement emphasising free markets to reduce poverty has found expression in the 'bottom of the pyramid' approach in recent years. It views the poor as 'resilient and creative entrepreneurs and value-conscious consumers'. This false and romanticised view of the poor harms them in two ways. First, it undermines or under-emphasises the importance of legal, regulatory and social mechanisms to protect the poor who are vulnerable consumers. Second, it over-emphasises micro-credit and under-emphasises fostering modern enterprises that can generate employment opportunities for the poor. More importantly, it grossly under-emphasises the critical role and responsibility of the state in poverty reduction.

Sir, I feel targeting the poor as a market is causing them to wastefully spend part of their already meagre income on low priority products and services. Like your vision of PURA for the villages, another vision is needed to enrich the people at the bottom of the community pyramid in urban areas rather than persuading them to buy sachets of shampoos and other such products which they can well do without.

The poor are poor not because they are untrained or illiterate but because they cannot retain the returns of their labour. They have no control over their livelihood, and it is the ability to sustain their existence that gives people the power to rise out of poverty
– Muhammad Yunus

The primary objective of PURA (Providing Urban Amenities in Rural Areas) is to create sustainable development in the rural areas. PURA will empower the people in the villages with increased employment opportunities, using their traditional core competencies combined with sufficient value addition and necessary skill upgradation, thereby enhancing their per capita income to at least twice the existing level. Hence the question of the poor remaining poor is not relevant in PURA.

I am happy that you like the vision of PURA. You have asked what can be the vision to enrich the people at the bottom of the community pyramid in urban areas. There are many national initiatives at the ground level using suitable technologies to protect the environment and bring about sustainable development. Some of these are : providing safe drinking water and water for irrigation; reducing pollution levels; increasingly adopting renewable energy resources to reduce dependency on fossil fuels; managing the natural resources so that there is no environment degradation leading to further deterioration of health and environment; and enriching the bio-diversity thereby bringing peace and economic prosperity to the nation. But the question remains, how would all this benefit the poor and make their lives better. How can the poor become the beneficiaries of sustainable development?

With the help of science and technology, we have been using natural resources such as sea, land, rivers, mountains and forests for human and economic development. But in doing so, we have ended up polluting the environment. There are very high levels of carbon dioxide emissions into the atmosphere, there is widespread deforestation, and unchecked pollution of the land, sea and river because of dumping untreated industrial and municipal waste coupled with indiscriminate use of chemical fertilizers and pesticides. Today, our natural resources are dwindling and the polluted environment is leading to global warming and climate changes. The irony is that those who own the industries based on these natural resources and reap its economic benefits live far away in the safety of their comfortable homes; and it is the local people living in the nearby areas who bear the brunt of the actual collateral costs in terms of environment degradation and accidents which may, and sometimes do, occur. Costs of such environmental degradation are not always limited to the local people but may even end up impacting people across states. The result is that the entire nation suffers. What we need is sustainable development in every aspect of the use of our natural resources which is essential in promoting and protecting the environment.

The convergence of technologies such as bio-technology, informatics, and nano-technology and eco-technologies offer the hope to realise multiple products and systems in water, energy, environment, management of pollution, waste and biodiversity and healthcare. For example, solar technology has provided the first 700 MW solar park in one of our states, nano-filter technology is being used to find safe drinking water solutions, nano packaging and eco-technologies are providing bio-degradable packaging solutions. Research and development are progressing, using the convergence of these technologies, to provide clean and green products to humanity. The question is how to ensure that these technologies benefit the poor and the marginalised?

The benefits of these can be transmitted to the poorer sections through the use of information and communication technology. Information collection, generation and dissemination through terrestial communication networks and satellite networking has attained new dimensions due to the convergence of geo-spatial technologies. This helps to monitor and track the natural resources and plan for improving the environment and enriching the biodiversity. Information and communications systems will collect data from land and space through the terrestrial network and wireless technologies, and data mining and its analysis will transform this data into knowledge.

The Geographic Information Systems, Global Positioning Systems and geo-spatial technologies using satellite networks may acquire and analyse the data from remote sensing, resource mapping equipment on land, water and sea, movement and path of the river dimensions through satellites such as Cartosat and Oceansat. Modern geo-spatial analytical tools may analyse the data generated which may enrich the knowledge on how to bring sustainable development in multiple areas such as management of waste, pollution, energy, mobility and bio-diversity. Using information and communication technologies, we need to evolve an innovative societal business model so that the research results of convergence of technologies are used for human development in a sustainable way.

But evolving an innovative business model, which will take the technologies to the users for creating sustainable development systems, remains a largely unaddressed issue. A unique societal

Societal Developmental Radar for tracking empowerment attributes

business model, which would empower and enrich the end-users such as farmers, fishermen, skilled workers, people living in the rural areas, is yet to be evolved. When a sustainable development societal business model is put into practise it will result in the optimal use of available natural resources, their recycling without polluting the environment thus ensuring its availability for the future generations.

We need to establish a Societal Developmental Radar to review and monitor how the user community pyramid has benefited the users. I suggest eight essential empowerment attributes which are critical to the realisation of our goal of a happy, prosperous and peaceful society beginning at the base of the pyramid. These attributes are: access to food and water, access to healthcare, access to income generation capacity, access to education and capacity building, access to quality power and communication applications, state of societal conflict, access to financial services, access to clean and green environment.

We can have three targets for the achievement of these eight attributes; one, the current status of these attributes, two, the medium-term target and three, the long-term target with specific time schedules. Societal transformers and corporates through Corporate Social Responsibility can deploy the applications of the technologies they are developing to empower the people living at the bottom of the user community pyramid and the outcome may be tracked and monitored through the Societal Development Radar. India can never be a developed country until we learn to recognise the rights of the poor and give them basic amenities and sustained livelihoods through the needs of the Developmental Radar. A tree will not grow unless its roots are nurtured with water and nutrients in the soil.

New skills
for a new generation

Q Sir, I heard your inspiring lecture at the Uttar Pradesh Development Conclave. Uttar Pradesh is the largest state of India, home to a fifth of our population and every seventh Lok Sabha member comes from here. If that were not enough, this gargantuan state has also produced eight of the thirteen duly elected Prime Ministers of our country. But over the years it has lost some of its political clout and is no longer in a position to influence the national agenda.

The state remains locked in its worst ever caste and community clashes. The politicians of this state do not have even a catchy slogan to offer, forget about any blueprint for change. It is no more a fight between ideologies. All the political parties in the state are only interested in configuring the right mix of social engineering to forge a winning caste coalition. **None of the political parties talk of better governance or providing jobs for the unemployed but are concerned about only caste and community affiliations.**

The situation is worsening. My question to you is, how can this divisiveness be overcome?

A candle loses nothing by lighting another candle
– James Keller

Uttar Pradesh is a very big state. It is home to 200 million people and its problems are in plenty and difficult to solve. I can understand your anxiety about the ongoing political dynamics but in a healthy democracy it is normal to have such upheavals.

Rich in both human and natural resources, Uttar Pradesh (UP) had earlier positioned itself as the pace-setter for India's economic and social development. Most of the state falls in the fertile Indo-Gangetic plain, with high natural soil fertility, abundant rainfall, and surface and groundwater resources. The western region was the springboard for the Green Revolution in the 1960s and 1970s and this helped the state move away from its previously low levels of agricultural growth. Accompanied by steady reductions in poverty levels between the late 1970s and 1980s, growth accelerated, and purposeful investments in agricultural research, irrigation, roads and marketing infrastructure fuelled further advances in the 1980s. But economic growth faltered in the 1990s and has fallen behind that of India's better performing states. While a recent acceleration in growth suggests that the deterioration in performance has been arrested, but many problems still remain.

Poverty, measured in terms of material deprivation, is high in UP relative to other Indian states, and progress at reducing poverty has been uneven over the past two decades. The vast majority of poor households live in rural areas and historically, poverty has been concentrated in the eastern and southern regions of the state. The people of Uttar Pradesh suffer from a high burden of disease. Maternal mortality rate is high, at more than 300 deaths per 1,00,000 live births, compared to 178 in India as a whole. Children are particularly vulnerable: they are frequently malnourished, and over half the children under three years of age are significantly underweight and less shielded against childhood diseases. Three out of ten children have never been immunized, and the infant mortality rate in UP, more than 50 per 1000 live births, is among the highest in India. Infant mortality is particularly high in households suffering from high levels of material deprivation.

In combating poverty the state will need to build on assets in the public and private sector and also the real and potential assets of the poor themselves

Poverty is the result of low levels of assets, combined with low and uncertain returns. In combating poverty, the state will need to build purposefully on all its assets, those in public hands as well as those in the private sector, and the real and potential assets of the poor themselves. The labour of the poor is concentrated in low-paid casual daily wage work as most own little or no land or productive assets. Poor people lack marketable skills and, in most cases, also lack literacy; they suffer disproportionately from poor health and disability. In the absence of skills and start-up capital, poor men and women are ill-equipped to take advantage of the opportunities provided by growth in the economy.

At the UP Development Conclave in May 2012, I proposed the launch of a comprehensive skill-based empowerment mission in the state. I recommended setting up 1,00,000 social enterprises across the state. Each of these social enterprises could employ about 50 social entrepreneurs drawn from the large pool of the educated unemployed youth. In the presence of the Chief Minister, Shri Akhilesh Yadav, I said, "These social entrepreneurs of Uttar Pradesh can work with the communities at the grass root level along the developmental radar. This will help find value-added employment for the 25 lakh unemployed and underemployed youth in the state and open avenues for additional growth."

In the absence of skills and start-up capital the poor are ill-equipped to take advantage of the opportunities provided by growth in the economy

For example, such a social enterprise can take up the task of procuring local raw materials, say mangoes from Malihabad, and process them into nutritionally-fortified foods and make them available to the masses with a priority for the local markets and with only the necessary minimum margins on price. This way, the social entrepreneur can be the bridge among local products, local nutritional needs, technology and marketing. Emphasising on the need to develop important cities such as Lucknow, Kanpur,

Noida and Meerut, I suggested the state government could also set up a UP Skill Enterprise Corporation with a private-public partnership model which can identify young talent in traditional skills in colleges and shop-floors and invest in them to groom them as entrepreneurs.

At the root of divisiveness is the problem of scarcity of resources

Through targeted training of the youth across Industrial Training Institutes, youth workshops, marketing technological process enhancements and other interventions, the entire state can benefit. Each district can clearly identify its unique skill-sets, its potential, and how to go about achieving the mission of developing an economy based around the local products and skills. Also, they can benchmark themselves against one another and find marketing avenues and distribution support. This will lead to the formation of industrial hubs in many areas, including Badohi, Moradabad, Aligarh, Agra and Sonebhadra. So, friend, this is an alternative agenda for governance and economic development as given to the political system of the state.

Two key factors that determine a community's ability to manage its resources are its social cohesion and willingness to set and strive for common goals

You have asked how divisiveness of caste and community can be overcome. At the root of this divisiveness is the problem of scarcity of resources. Poor people often depend more heavily on forest resources to meet their subsistence needs than do people who are wealthier. Poor people, for example, may not be able to afford gas for cooking or modern medicines. Instead, they depend on forest products for fuel and medicine. Because of this, they may face very different incentives for use of the natural resources and therefore, they may have strong opinions about what the rules for access and exploitation of natural resources should be.

The two key factors that determine a community's ability to manage resources are its social cohesion and willingness to set and strive for common goals. This does not mean that the community must be homogeneous. Social identities in Indian society are not going to vanish. Also, there are many communities of people with the same ethnicity, religion, family and history that are deeply divided. Conversely, there are many heterogeneous communities made up of people of varying backgrounds who are nevertheless able to overcome their differences in order to work towards common objectives. The key issue is whether the community is able to establish common goals and strategies for accomplishing those goals, and then work together.

In the 2014 General Elections, India's voting transcended caste and community boundaries. Even the secular-communal divide was rendered irrelevant. There is hope in the air. India has voted for development, for faster growth, creation of jobs, and control of inflation. Sustainable development will melt away all divisions and from the fusion of various metals of religions, regions, castes and communities, a strong alloy of India would emerge.

When can
I sing a song of India

Q Your lecture, 'When can I sing a song of India', is indeed very inspiring. But the inspiration is fleeting. In less than three years after its introduction, the future of the low-cost indigenously developed tablet computer, 'Akash', looks uncertain, even though the government is trying to rescue it. Its very relevance has been put to question by the sudden rise of competing low-cost tablets from private companies. The same thing happened to the 'Chitra' heart valve, the low cost indigenously developed stent. Is it yet another lesson for India that, to achieve socially desirable results in a developing nation, noble intentions are usually not as efficient as the natural forces of materialism, corporate self-interest and the market? Bill Gates has said that India has to focus on providing basic infrastructure before worshipping the computer. A few months ago, in Uttar Pradesh, which has a sub-Saharan quality of life, the Chief Minister, along with his wife stood on a stage and, gave away free laptops to high school students, much in the manner of giving alms. He has promised to give away more.

Tell me, Sir, will the song of India be a duet of extreme poverty and the worship of digital technology?

Unless India stands up to the world, no one will respect us. In this world, fear has no place. Only strength respects strength ·
– APJ Abdul Kalam

I can feel your pain about the state of affairs in our country. It is natural for a righteous, peace-loving citizen to feel concerned about the future. Before I answer your question, let me share with you my three visions of our country.

In the three thousand years of our history, people from all over the world have come and invaded us, captured our lands and ruled over us. From Alexander onwards, the Greeks, the Portuguese, the British, the French, the Dutch, all of them came and plundered our wealth, our resources, and took over what was naturally ours. Yet we have not done this to any nation. We have not conquered anyone. We have not grabbed their land, overrun their culture or tried to enforce our way of life on them. Why? We did not invade other lands or subjugate other people because we respect the freedom of human beings, ours, as well of others. Therefore my first vision of India is that of freedom.

My second vision for India is that of development. For the last sixty-seven years we have been a developing nation. It is time we see ourselves become a developed nation. We are amongst the top five nations of the world in terms of Gross Domestic Product. We have a 5 per cent growth rate in most areas. Our poverty levels are falling and our achievements are being globally recognised today. Yet we lack the self-confidence

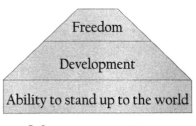

My three visions of India

to see ourselves as a developed nation, self-reliant and self-assured. We need to change this.

My third vision is that India must stand up to the world. Because I believe that unless India stands up to the world, no one will respect us. Only strength respects strength. We must be strong not only as a military power but also as an economic power. Both must go hand in hand.

For the transformation of our nation into an economically developed country, I have identified five areas, based on India's core competencies, natural resources and talented manpower, to accelerate the growth rate of GDP. These five areas are: agriculture and food processing aimed at doubling the present production of agriculture and food processing; infrastructure with reliable electric power providing urban amenities to rural areas, and increasing solar power operations; education and healthcare directed towards illiteracy, social security, and overall health for the population; information and communication technology to promote e-governance, education in remote areas, telecommunication, and telemedicine; and finally critical technologies and strategic industries for the growth of nuclear technology, space technology and defence technology.

The country's youth can make a difference to society in the areas of literacy, environment and social justice and towards minimising the rural-urban divide. It is very important that Developed India be a nation where there is equitable distribution and adequate

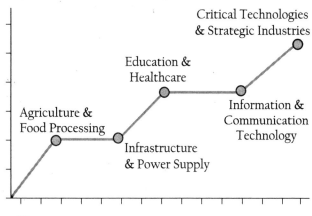

Focus areas for accelerating India's GDP growth rate

access to energy and quality water, where agriculture, industry and service sector work together in symphony, a nation where the best of healthcare is available to all, where the governance is responsive, transparent and corruption-free.

Now I come to your question, will the song of India, be a duet of extreme poverty and the worship of digital technology? My answer is no. Of course there is hard work ahead. We must give up all our little quarrels and differences because these quarrels are absolutely wrong. Our scriptures condemn these quarrels. Our forefathers and those great men from whom we claim our descent and whose blood is in our veins, will look down with contempt on their children quarrelling about petty differences.

With the giving up of quarrels, improvements in all areas will follow. Where the lifeblood is strong and pure, no disease-carrying germs can live in that body. Our lifeblood is our spirituality. If it flows clear, if it flows strong and pure and vigorous, everything will be right; political, social, any other material defects, even the poverty of the land, can all be cured.

To take a simile from modern medicine, we know that there must be one of the two causes to produce a disease, an external disease-carrying germ or virus and the internal state or health of the body. There is no power in any germ to cause a disease in a healthy body. It is only when the body is degraded to a low level of vitality that it allows the germs to enter, thrive and multiply. In fact, millions of germs are continually passing through our body, but so long as our body is healthy and fit, it is never conscious of them. It is only when the body is weak, that these germs take possession of it and produce disease. Such is the case with national life.

It is only when the national 'body' is weak that all sorts of disease germs whether of a political, social, educational or intellectual nature are able to make an entry into the nation's system and cause disease

It is only when the national 'body' is weak that all sorts of disease germs, whether of a political, social, educational or intellectual nature, are able to make an entry into the nation's system and cause disease. To remedy it, therefore, we must go to the root of this disease and cleanse the blood of all impurities. By making the blood pure and the body vigorous, it will have the strength to resist and throw off all external disease-germs.

We have seen that our vigour, our strength, in fact, our very national life is in our spiritual nature. I am not going to discuss whether it is right or not, whether it is correct or not, whether it is beneficial or not in the long run to have this vitality in spirituality. But the fact is that it is there; we cannot get out of it, we have it now and forever, and we have to stand by it, even if some of us have not the same faith in it that I have.

We, as a nation, are bound in our spirituality, and if we give it up, we will be smashed to pieces. Spirituality is the life of our nationhood and it must be strengthened. We have withstood the shocks of centuries simply because we took great care of it and sacrificed everything else for it. Our forefathers underwent everything boldly, even death itself, but preserved their traditions of spirituality and compassion.

The Indian mind, first and foremost, is spiritual, and then anything else. So this spirituality has to be strengthened. How do we do it? It can be done by being righteous. By being pure, you can have all the power. When you are righteous, you will find that others instinctively cooperate with you. Positive circumstances will begin to emerge almost as if from nowhere. Something, almost mysterious, will emanate from you that will make others want to follow you, listen to you and subconsciously, even against their will, carry out your plans.

Now is the time to decide your future, while you possess the energy of youth, not when you are worn-out and jaded, but in the freshness and vigour of youth. This is the time for work; for the freshest and the untouched flowers alone are to be laid at the feet of Mother India. Rouse yourselves,

We as a nation are bound in our spirituality and if we give it up we will be smashed to pieces Spirituality is the life of our nationhood and it must be strengthened

therefore, for life is short. Though life is short, the soul is immortal and eternal, and death being certain, let us therefore take up a great ideal and dedicate our whole life to it. Let this be your determination.

Competing with the world

The iron bird

Q Sir, you cannot be unaware of the erosion of our industrial base and the fact that Chinese goods are flooding our markets. You cannot be unaware of the shift to a service economy that favours the better educated, which means that schools are becoming the primary policy instrument for enhancing both social mobility and our competitive position. You cannot be unaware that we must improve our stock of human capital, that the PIN code you are born into shouldn't determine your destiny, as all too often it does. You cannot be unaware of the fact that our economic and social policy, has been suborned by the greed of the powerful few, rather than being driven by doing maximum good for the maximum number of people.

While the private sector continues to form thousands of start-ups that keep us at the cutting edge of many of the emerging technologies, the government continues to create many hurdles. There are intolerable delays at all levels of government clearances. On an average it takes almost two years, a lifetime in the technolgy world, to obtain the necessary environmental, health, and safety permits to set up an industrial plant or factory.

Sir, when you talk about the 'I-can-do' spirit, it sounds unrealistic, at least, in the system that we are in today. Is there a way out? What use is it to talk about the way ahead to reach a distant future if we do not know the way out of our present prison?

Few things in the world are more powerful than a positive push - a smile, a word of optimism, hope and a 'I can do it' when things are tough
– Richard deVos

I share your concern about the flood-like presence of Chinese goods in our markets which is undermining our small and medium size industry, and putting pressure on the value of the Rupee. It should not have been allowed to happen in the first place, but it is never too late to correct the situation. Your observation on a vicious circle of delays and clearances in hindering indigenous industry from blossoming is also correct to an extent. The success of small start-ups is a combination of two factors, one, the entrepreunerial spirit of individuals and two, an environment conducive to the growth of this spirit. Agreed, that there are severe shortcomings in the environment, but let there be no doubt about the power of the 'I-can-do' spirit of us Indians. I am saying this from personal experience and let me share with you an incident that took place in 1998.

Let there be no doubt about the power of the 'I-can-do' spirit of Indians

In the early nineties, I was working on a project to develop an indigenous Light Combat Aircraft (LCA). The project team had decided to use the digital Fly-by-Wire Control System (FCS). As we did not have experience in developing FCS, we signed a contract with Lockheed Martin, USA for its development, as they had the experience in designing digital fly-by-wire system for F-16 fighter aircraft. The contract for the joint development of fly-by-wire system progressed smoothly between 1992-98. The defence and finance ministries, along with our technologists were constantly monitoring and providing an impetus to the progress of the project. Then on 11 May 1998, India carried out its nuclear test and the American government imposed technological sanctions against us. Due to these sanctions, the joint development with Lockheed Martin came to an abrupt stop. They even retained all the Indian equipment, software and the technical information, which were in their premises. This was a huge shock and setback for us.

I called for a meeting of the directors of the various laboratories involved in the project such as Prof IG Sharma, a renowned control system specialist at the Indian Institute of Science, Bangalore, Prof TK Goshal, a noted digital control system expert at Jadavpur University, and specialists from Defence Research and Development Organisation, Indian Space Research Organsiation and Hindustan Aeronautics Limited along with our financial advisors. After prolonged deliberations, the team came up with a plan by which the development of the FCS could be completed and the system certified for flight trials, without the support of Lockheed Martin.

We created an innovative test rig to enable the ground testing of the LCA-FCS in open and close-loop modes and also with the pilot in the loop. We named this test rig the Iron Bird. The test facility contained all the sub-systems like the cockpit, avionics suite, the outside window imagery and all other sub-systems, which interface with the heart of the LCA-FCS, the Digital Flight Control Computer (DFCC). The aim was to identify potential problems in any of the systems at the earliest instance, so that solutions could be found.

A large number of iterative Iron Bird tests were carried out for thousands of hours before the formal testing. The pilot flew the simulator for more than two thousand hours. Thus, what we missed from the foreign partner, we compensated by enhancing the joint development within the country, the critical design review, and increasing the test time to ensure safe man-rated design of the integrated flight control system. The entire team took the imposition of the sanction as a national challenge. They said if it would have taken three years with the support of Lockheed Martin, independently, they would do it in two years. If it was originally going to cost twenty million dollars, they would bring it down to ten million dollars. All this was done within the government framework involving highly experienced engineers, technocrats and academicians in the country. In December 2013 the LCA attained the Initial Operational Clearance and in February 2014 it was tested over the Great Himalayas. The Final Operational

Clearance is expected by December 2014, after which it will be inducted into the Indian Air Force.

This event reassured me that no country can dominate us by imposing technological or economic sanctions. The collective power of our scientific, managerial and financial expertise can defeat challenges from any nation.

Coming back to the issue of Chinese goods invading our markets, we need a national leadership with courage and confidence, to bring a level playing field in the industry and manufacturing sector. This would create an innovative, responsive eco-system which will empower the Indian industries with technology, funding and an environment for growth with inclusive public policies.

We need a national leadership with courage and confidence to bring a level playing field in industry and manufacturing sector by creating an innovative and responsive eco-system which will empower Indian industries

India can be a superpower in the twenty-first century, and this is not merely a dream or a vision. The foundation for this has already been laid, and if each one of us commits to build upon this foundation, then, surely in the coming years we will see a superpower India.

The dragon and the peacock

Q Sir, I read the lecture, 'Livable planet earth', which you gave in Beijing. Sir, it sounds hollow to me. I am sure you realise that in geopolitical matters, there is no futuristic thinking in India. The quality of our thinking and analysis is rather poor. Our leaders are self-enamoured of their wishful thinking. Someone once said that power and influence are not given, they are taken. China has shown how to take it. India does not seem to have the political will and courage to fight for it and take it.

The hope, that India might overtake China one day in economic growth, now seems a very distant one. But that comparison is not what should worry Indians most. The far greater gap between India and China is in the provision of essential public services, a failing that depresses living standards and is a persistent drag on growth. Inequality is high in both countries, but China has done far more than India to raise life expectancy, expand general education and secure healthcare for its people. India has elite schools of varying degrees of excellence for the privileged few. Among all Indians of the age seven-years or older, nearly one in every five males, and one in every three females, is illiterate. Most government schools are of low quality; even after four years of schooling less than half the children can divide 20 by 5. Of course, our strength in India is our deep-rooted democracy. In China, decision-making takes place at the top without any consensus building. What is needed, Sir, is a combination of democracy with leadership possessing a fast decision-making process.

Tell me, Sir, when will our leaders wake up to this reality? Before you show us the dream of livable planet, tell us how to live a decent life in India.

We must keep in mind the bottom line, working for the best, but preparing for the worst
– APJ Abdul Kalam

There are two contrasting views in both Beijing and New Delhi. One point of view is that each of the two emerging powers would fight for dominance in the Asian continent. It tends to describe relations between the two countries as hostile which could even lead to military confrontations or at least to a greater militarisation of the region. Both countries have nuclear weapons and are increasing and modernising their capabilities of conventional warfare. War is contained only because both realise the magnitude of loss that would take place if a nuclear war were to be unleashed. The second school of thought takes a liberal perspective, viewing China and India as two major emerging markets in an increasingly interdependent world where trade and commerce sustain peaceful co-existence. Going by our media it seems that the 'China threat theory' is the more dominant and perceived view.

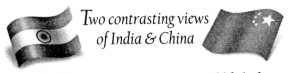

*Two contrasting views
of India & China*

*Each of the two emerging powers would fight for
dominance in the Asian continent*

*They are the two major emerging markets in an
increasingly interdependent world*

It is true that in direct comparison, we lag far behind China in almost all socio-economic indices. Western, and even some Indian experts, blame the slow democratic process for this situation. One has to keep in mind that India's political system is characterised by an enormous complexity due to the diversity of regions, people and opportunities which leads to blockages, leakages, idleness and corruption at all levels. But India's development has been quite stable without any major political upheavals.

In contrast, the Chinese model of development evolved after decades of social and economic turmoil. China had the Mao era, the Cultural Revolution, the post-Cultural Revolution and post-Tiananmen Square period. The transitions to these different phases were accompanied by major social and political unrests. India's federal democratic system, with all its flaws, has proved to be better to deal with social movements and turbulences until now. Independent India's economic performance till the 1990s, although with a low growth rate, was constant and predictable, while the Chinese political and economic situation was unstable and the social situation, at times, becoming even explosive. There can be no two opinions on the need for India to put all its efforts and resources to make up as quickly as possible on the lagging socio-economic indicators so that the benefits of growth and development reach all segments of society.

And while we look at developments within our own geographical boundaries, we also need to raise our vision to look at the bigger picture wherein all countries can co-exist on the planet Earth and how it can be sustained. We need a great vision which looks beyond individuals, ideologies, party affiliations, political ambitions and the present technological superiority. As long as there are inequities of development between regions, between urban and rural areas, between neighbouring countries in sharing valuable resources, peace will elude us. Modern technology has made the world a global village and this is leading to less tolerance for inequities. We have to use the same technology to provide economic development to the nation states and simultaneously assure peace on the planet. Hence, while creating wealth within national boundaries, we need to find new ways to ensure the viability and sustainability of the entire humankind and our planet. For this, humanity needs a great vision to forget its conflicts and move towards a common goal of peace and prosperity for all global citizens.

The European nations fought for a hundred years but then they got together and formed the European Union. It is true that India and China had a bad experience in 1962, but should we continue always using that as our reference point or guiding post? We have to decide, do we want cooperation or confrontation? Defence of our borders is of course very important and its integrity must be protected, but if we combine the population of India and China we are talking about 37 per cent of the world's population, and that offers a great opportunity.

There are huge opportunities for the two countries if they can come around and work for peace and prosperity, beginning with some specific projects

I have come to the conclusion that we should become a Master Civilization by coming together. There is tremendous potential if the two countries can come up with a joint vision which would encompass joint effort for a technology mission or a societal development mission or even multiple missions. There are huge opportunities for the two if they can come around and work for peace and prosperity, beginning with some specific projects, where we could be partners. This could become a harbinger for evolving a great model of cooperation in an integrated and unique way for nations to assimilate and arrive at world peace and prosperity for all.

In November 2012, I went to China on an invitation of the Peking University, Beijing, to address the Beijing Forum 2012. The theme of my speech was, "Evolution of the peaceful and prosperous planet earth", and I called for setting up a World Knowledge Platform for Global Action that would invest $4 billion to bring together universities, governments and entrepreneurs to take forward joint initiatives on sustainable development, renewable energy and the environment. The youth, the intellectuals, the academia and even those in the political field could appreciate the necessity for the two countires to work together. India could leverage China's core competencies in manufacturing while India could offer its know-how in IT and services.

I think there cannot be a greater vision for the nations other than to work together for transforming our world into the 'Livable Planet Earth'. That means we are leaving a sustainable world, where we have taken less from nature than what we have given to it, and thus securing the future for the generations to come.

What worked
yesterday won't work today

Q There is growing evidence of the beginnings
of an international economic order based on
electronic money. Big corporations are coming
together as a one-world government, and all
countries including USA and USSR, seem to be
toeing their line. Recently, it was reported in the
media that how USA had been clandestinely
indulging in electronic monitoring and surveillance
of the activities of not only the common people
but also of top ranking politicians across the world.
Though this created a huge uproar nobody knows
what is happening to this now. Has it been stopped
or is it still continuing? Backed by such powers
of electronic surveillance and control, will we see
the emergence of a supreme world leader who will
preside over the new unified one-world and a one-
world religion coordinating all the world's religions,
cults, faith groups and spiritual beliefs?

What is your take on the emerging new world order? Where would India fit into it? Are we going to be slaves again?

A thought is a cosmic order waiting to happen.
− Stephen Richards

We are living through an exciting and uncertain transition to a new era where, probably, a global 'tipping point' is being reached. Such historic shifts require that mindsets and paradigms through which we analyse and understand this world, as well as plan and act within it, must be 'reloaded' to adjust to new realities.

Recently, on a trip to the United States, I was told that most of the controls of the aircraft in which I was flying were software driven and probably developed in India. In another instance, when I presented my credit card, I was told that it was being processed in a back-end server located in Mauritius. Similarly, once when I visited a software development centre in Bangalore, I was fascinated to find that it truly presented a multicultural environment: a software developer from China working under a project leader from Korea along with a software engineer from India and a hardware architect from the US and a communication expert from Germany, were all working together to solve a problem for a bank located in Australia.

You expressed the fear that a new world order is being implemented by the cult of intelligence at the core of the surveillance-industrial complex through mass surveillance and the use of Social Security numbers, bar-coding of retail goods with Universal Product Code markings, and, most recently, RFID (Radio Frequency Identification) tagging via microchip implants. I understand your anxiety but let me reassure you that it is not going to happen.

But first you must understand the reason for this paranoia or anxiety. The paranoia about technology which is capable of mind control, population control, surveillance abuse to aid big business and governments arises from a combination of two factors, namely, strong individualistic values and lack of power. The first

What worked yesterday won't work today

Yesterday	Today
Natural resources defined power	Knowledge is power
Hierarchy was the model	Synergy is the mandate
Leaders commanded & controlled	Leaders empower and coach
Shareholders came first	Customers come first
Employees took orders	Teams make decisions
Seniority signified status	Creativity drives status
Production determined availability	Competitiveness is the key
Value was extra	Value is everything
Everyone was a competitor	Everyone is a customer
Profits were earned through expediency	Work with integrity and succeed with integrity

attribute refers to people who care deeply about their individual rights and living their lives without interference or obligations to a larger system like the government. When this is combined with a sense of powerlessness in their own lives they suffer from intense anxiety about an apparent loss of autonomy to outside forces or regulators. When fervent individualists feel that they cannot exercise their independence, they experience a crisis and assume that larger forces are to blame for usurping this freedom.

In this context I would like to quote from Ayn Rand's book, *Atlas Shrugged*, 'I am not primarily an advocate of capitalism, but of egoism; I am not primarily an advocate of egoism, but of reason. If one recognises the supremacy of reason and applies it consistently, all the rest follows. When I disagree with a rational man, I let reality be our final arbiter; if I am right, he will learn; if I am wrong, I will; one of us will win, but both will profit.'

The action required to sustain human life is primarily intellectual: everything man needs has to be discovered by his mind and produced by his effort. The world in the twenty-first century will be, more than ever before, a knowledge-based society. I was reading a book, *Empires of the Mind* by Denis Waitley. This book describes the world as it was yesterday and what it is today and which is presented on page 220.

If intellect and knowledge are the source of all power, and both these reside in individuals and given that individuals are valuing their freedoms more than ever before, a scenario as you are painting is not likely to materialise. Also, the power of any one individual through the multiplier effect of the Internet will act as a bulwark against a 'one-world-order'.

At the same time, there are movements taking place at regional levels which also will prevent a one-world order becoming a reality. Instead of the two traditional superpowers, USA and USSR, there will be multiple power centres such as BRICS. The concept and the emerging reality of BRICS (Brazil, Russia, India, China, and South Africa) as a geopolitical and economic grouping of nations introduces a new dynamic to global governance and economic relations. The BRICS nations represent 42 per cent of the world's population and 18 per cent of global GDP.

China's economy, after three decades of 10 per cent expansion, massive foreign investment in agriculture and industry, and recent domestic market-led growth has lifted some four hundred million people out of poverty and is creating a middle class at a phenomenal rate. It has seen urbanisation approaching seventeen million people a year.

India, with its established democracy and despite its massive rural poverty, has succeeded in creating an economic miracle led by technology and services that has laid the foundation for long term sustainable growth and put India as one of the forefront nations of BRICS.

Brazil has come into its own as the leading Latin American economy. It is finding synergy with China in joint ventures based on an exchange of natural resources and oil for low-cost manufactured goods.

Russia, likewise, possesses a formidable economy, partly due to its role as a leading oil and gas producer. Its potential as a trade partner and expertise in science and technology makes Russia a valuable ally for fellow BRICS members.

The inclusion of South Africa as the fifth member of the BRICS group ensures that Africa has a rightful place in global financial, developmental, and trade architecture.

As for a one-world religion coordinating all the world's religions, cults, faith groups and spiritual beliefs, I see an increase in the number of people drawing on both Eastern and Western spiritual and metaphysical traditions and infusing them with influences from self-help and motivational psychology and holistic health practices.

While on the one hand we are seeing increasing power centres of blocs of countries and business corporations, at the same time, the increasing power and reach of any one individual to impact the global scenario will act as a balance on the former.

❑❑❑

What readers are saying about this book *

"I just loved the book. Truly inspirational. It depicts how we should come up with ideas to mend one's future towards the bright side."

—Kavya Reddy (Hyderabad, India)

"Really a good book at an affordable price! Contains good messages for life."

—Sriram Praveen S

"Really enjoyed reading it. I will read it again and again as long as I live!"

—Sathya Narayanan K (Chennai, India)

"Really it is the best guideline for our youth. This book means a lot to me, and I love it, I found it as the best book I ever read."

—Premanand

"A must read book and the very best for a New Year gift to your loved ones, particularly to any young child!"

—Sandeepan Goswami (Guwahati, India)

"Its a masterstroke by Dr. Kalam. The book is a collection of 32 questions that The Missile Man has been asked repeatedly by millions of his young fans and followers. As he gives the answers to the questions, I am sure you will relate to almost every question. The questions vary from, How to get success?, How to make a better society? How to empower women? to How can India become a Super Power? Every person irrespective of age should read this amazing work of Dr. Kalam."

—Sanghi Irani

"A well written book and greatly enjoyed reading the book."

—Kaizad Mistri (Pune, India)

"Abdul Kalam's advice on many common problems is amazing."

—Harish

"Many things to get from this book....must read."

—Hiren Patel
